Reviewers on Amazon have said

***** 'This is a great read...in the of her inner self she hadn't known existed. It is both educational - I learnt so much about the Shetland Isles history and folklore and is startlingly emotionally honest. The tone is intimate, and full of warmth and humour. Thoroughly recommended. I was sorry when I came to the end.' - *Wendy Evans, Counsellor*

**** 'Like a mini Welsh/Scottish version of the alchemist. A journey of self-discovery. Of going away and finding the treasure was at home...' - S. Murphy, RAF

***** 'I really like the way this author thinks, writes and feels about her experiences... Her story is patient, emotional and down to earth and touched with hidden truths and insights into an island world that most of us 'non islanders' would know very little about... At times very poignant and touching and as a first memoir, it is a fine one. I look forward to more stories and adventures from this author in the future.' - Sue Seifert, Writer

***** 'Janet gave me a yearning to visit these islands, then very quickly, with the use of her descriptive, witty and analytical writing I felt as if I had lived there with her and her husband. An honest, insightful, humorous and informative read.' - Denise Hayward, Trainer

***** 'An engaging, romantic and humorous journey into the landscape of the Shetland Isles, its culture, environment and people'... 'I laughed and cried as I travelled the length and breadth of the fascinating human and environmental landscapes portrayed in this saga.' - Diana Wallace, Snr Social Worker

Janet Teal Daniel

Shetland Saga

A Soothmoother's Story

Copyright © Janet Teal Daniel 2015

Copyright © 2015 by Janet Teal Daniel

ISBN: 978-1-326-42104-5

Published by www.publishandprint.co.uk

All rights reserved. No part of this book may be used or reproduced in any manner whatsoever without written permission from the author

Cover design: Dave Lewis

Acknowledgements:

I would like to thank all the Shetlanders and Soothmoothers* who generously welcomed, encouraged and supported us. We have changed the names of some of the principal players in our story to protect their identities

I would also like to thank Susan Richardson, my creative writing tutor, who encouraged and mentored me in the writing of this book

*A soothmoother or southmouther is anyone who resides south of the Shetlands

For Rhys

Synopsis

In 2004, Janet and Ieuan Rhys Daniel left their marital home of twenty-five years in South Wales to live and work in the Shetland Isles. This is the story of their experience and explores themes of attachment, relationships, connection, remoteness and belonging.

MAPS

1. British Isles indicating Taffs Well and Shetland

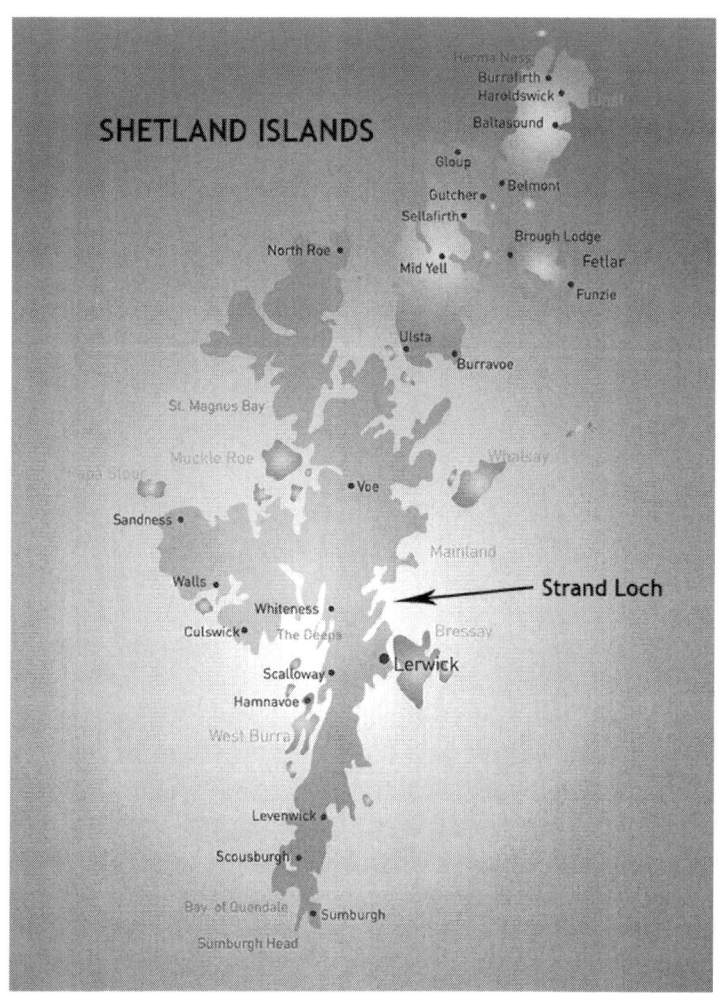

2. Shetland Isles, showing location of Strand Loch

Shetland Saga

A Soothmoother's Story

June 2004

'Want more than a new job?' read the job advert in Therapy: the U.K Journal for Counsellors and Psychotherapists in its Spring 2004 issue.
Yes I do.
The last four years had been interesting working with the Royal College of Nursing, but I was becoming bored and frustrated. The same problems again and again, underpaid, stressed out casualties of a National Health Service that wasn't working well for its staff.
I read on. 'Imagine working in a pollution free environment with low crime... never more than 3 miles from the sea, great leisure facilities, trout fishing, sailing and no traffic jams to hold you back'.
Sounds good.
'...wide range of cultural activities and fresh local food... if you would like to combine real career satisfaction with an exceptional quality of life, this could be the post you are looking for.'
It certainly sounds like it.

'Where's that?' had been the response of most of my friends when I told them about my forthcoming interview in Shetland. When I got the job, friends' comments ranged from 'You're brave,' 'mad' or 'bloody hell!'

The Shetland Isles is a chain of over one hundred islands, of which around sixteen are populated. They lie to the north east of Scotland, about 250miles from Aberdeen and stretch nearly 90miles from Muckle Flugga in the north to Fair Isle in the south. The Faroes and Bergen in Norway are almost equidistant from Lerwick.

Our two children had differing views of our plans. Our son Liam aged 19 was on his gap year. After school he had worked in the Alps, travelled to Thailand, Australia and New Zealand and was about to go off to university in England. He was full of encouragement. Our daughter Rachel was 23, and since leaving university had also done seasons working in the Alps, did a teaching English as a foreign language course in Prague and taught in Italy. She was still trying to find her career path. When I told her our news the phone line filled with meaningful silence.

'She's not saying but I know she's not happy about us going,' I said to Rhys my husband, when I came off the phone.

'Oh, I am coming then?'

'What do you mean?'

'You said, 'us' going. I thought you wanted to go alone.'

The other response from some Welsh people was, 'Is your husband going with you? What does he think about leaving Wales?' The last year or so had been a difficult one for us as a couple. We had been married and living together in Wales for almost twenty five years and like many couples whose children are leaving the nest we were forced to look at our relationship and renegotiate the terms of being together. Twelve years earlier, at aged fifty, Rhys had got a virus that took away his hearing completely in one ear and left him with raging tinnitus. It meant he had to give up his long career as Head of Art at a Welsh secondary school and for the past few years had done various part-time jobs, while trying to develop his own art work. I was the lead breadwinner and he provided day-to day care and support to the children and this arrangement had worked well for a long time. However, seeing the children go off having independent adventures made me feel restless. I had done the same at their age, volunteering in Indonesia, working for the British Council in Indonesia and Greece. I was now fifty-five, I wanted a gap year too and I needed some space. When I saw the advertisement for a counsellor in my professional journal I thought it might be the ideal opportunity to have both but as my start date got nearer I began to find it hard to imagine going to Shetland alone without

Rhys. My new job would be part of the newly established Shetland Primary Care Counselling Service, working in health centres in Lerwick, the largest town on the mainland and on two other small islands, Whalsay, to the east and Unst, the most northerly of all the British Isles. At my age I considered myself lucky to have been given this opportunity and I hadn't hesitated, until now.

'No, I would like you to come if you still want to.'

'Yes, I'm up for it,' he grinned.

Thank God for that. I'm starting to feel a bit panicky about the whole project.

'The job is permanent but perhaps we should go for a year and then review our situation.'

'Sounds good.'

'But we'll need you to get a job if you can.'

'O.K. I'll give it my best shot.'

Excellent.

'What about Rachel then?'

'I suppose she's anxious about her PGCE,' he replied. 'We won't be here for support.'

'Yes, you're right. The post-graduate teaching course in Cardiff has a reputation for being tough.'

'Do you think she's also worried about living in the house on her own?'

'Yes, but she said she'd rather live here than rent a room with other students and Liam has to have somewhere to come back to in the holidays.'
'Mmm.'
'Look, if we're going to manage the upkeep of this house and rent somewhere up there, we'll need a lodger. Anyway, she or he will be company for Rachel.'

Interviewing for the lodger proved challenging. Rachel, positioned her athletic frame hidden from view near the window with a good view of the front gate. As soon as the prospective lodger opened the gate and our daughter caught a glimpse she nodded her approval or disapproval to Rhys and I seated at the back of the room. Disapproval mainly. A couple of young women seemed suitable on paper but not in the flesh. Too this or too that. A middle aged hippy professor sweated more at his 'interview' with us than he probably did for his position with the university. He then spent a lot of time wandering around the house feeling its vibes. Later, he called to say he liked Rachel and the house but it was too far out from the university.

'He was too far out for me,' she said. 'In my mind I had already turned him down anyway.'
Will we ever find anyone suitable?
Finally, we interviewed Jen, a large jolly woman in her late twenties, who gave us reassurances on how she would manage the cleaning and any potential conflict between her and Rachel.
'Well?'

'I'm not sure. There's something about her,' she mused.

Oh for God's sake.

'At this rate we're not going to get anyone before we leave. Jen can provide references and a deposit. Sorry love, but done deal.'

Well, we are desperate.

Small Ferry Crossing

October 2004

A couple of weeks later we said goodbye to twenty-five years of family life in Taffs Well, a village five miles from Cardiff.

'When will I see you again?' asked our daughter mournfully, as we packed our old green Ford Escort Estate to the brim; winter and summer clothes, bikes, Rhys' art materials and boxes of stuff that might come in handy in our new rented home.

'I'm not sure, but I'll phone you every day and we'll meet up at Christmas,' I replied squeezing her to my bosom. She perked up a bit.

'Don't worry Mum and Dad. I will be fine.'
Yes dear, I want to believe that.

'Get going Rhys," I whispered. 'Otherwise I might change my mind.'

He put the car into first gear and revved away. We waved until our daughter had disappeared from view.

'I just hope we're doing the right thing,' I muttered.

'Mmm.'

We decided to take a few days on the drive up to Aberdeen, where we would be getting the Northlink ferry on to Shetland, a further 300 odd miles and 14hours away; nearer to Bergen in Norway than Aberdeen in Scotland.

We popped in to see Liam in halls in Loughborough University.

'I think it's great what you're doing,' he said as he showed us into his bedroom. His room had the slight tainted smell of aging trainers. He looked pale and tussle haired, like he'd just got up.

'Your liver managed to survive Freshers' week then?'

Liam gave me a crooked smile. Next to a poster of an extreme mountain biker in full flight I glimpsed a small photo of the family pinned on his notice board. My throat tightened.

'When will you come up to see us?' I asked as the three of us sat in a row on his single bed drinking tea from mugs I'd bought for him at Hypervalue.

It's the little things that kick start nostalgia isn't it?

'Next year probably.'

'What about Christmas?'

'I may go snowboarding.'

'Fine. No problem.'

This may be harder than I thought.

'Better get going if we're to arrive in Darlington by dinner time,' Rhys said.

'Take care and have a great time,' Liam shouted after us. 'I'll be fine. Don't worry about me.'

That's what your sister said.

We also dropped in to see old friends and family en-route to Aberdeen in Bromsgrove, Darlington and Edinburgh. They all parted with,

'Good Luck. Don't know when we'll see you again.'
Anyone would think we're going to the moon.

It was already getting dark when we embarked on the Northlink ferry, the Hjaltland, from Aberdeen one wet evening in mid October. It was a large modern vessel with plenty of cabin accommodation. Being cheapskates we decided to forgo the cost of a cabin, despite the coded warning of the cabin crew that it looked like being a rough crossing.

'Better take the sleeping bags up with us,' said Rhys, delving into the back seat. 'Can you remember where we packed them?'
You packed the car.

After getting half the boot out and putting it back we made our way up the stairs from the car deck to the passenger deck arms full of old camping equipment.

'It's like a cruise ship,' remarked Rhys, stroking the chrome handrail.

'Yes, it sure is.' My insides fluttered with excitement.

The reception area sparkled in highly polished surfaces, mirrors and reflected light. The welcome staff were smartly dressed in starched white shirts and shiny waistcoats. I caught a waft of fresh aftershave.

'Let's dump our stuff and have a drink to celebrate.'

'Good idea.'

A friendly Scottish voice directed us to a dimmed room which reminded me of the interior of an aircraft with rows of tip back seats. We dumped our stuff and went off to explore the ship. There was a buffet style restaurant, a dress for dinner eat the same food but cost you a fortune restaurant, a couple of bars, a children's play area, a gambling area, shop and cinema, all connected by long corridors with beautiful photographs of the Orkney and Shetland Isles; and stacks of paper bags discreetly placed in racks like new magazines waiting to be read.

After a fish and chip supper and a couple of glasses of wine we returned to the seated area and tried to bed down.

'I can't get comfortable, can you?' I whinged.

'No, it's my back. These seats don't go back far enough.'

The ship began to sway from side to side and rain hit the plastic windows like gravel thrown in to a cement mixer.

'There aren't many people in here. The car deck was full. Where is everybody?'

'Well, there are people in the bar, but it's noisy and smoky. Shall I have a look round and see if there are any free sofas to sleep on?'

'Thanks Rhys. That would be great.' I watched him sway up the central isle apologizing profusely for inadvertently grabbing one passenger's hair and falling

into the lap of another. A little later I watched him sway back.
I hope he's found somewhere.
'No luck I'm afraid. They are all taken.'
'Then I'm on the floor.'
I got down and tried to squeeze myself under the seat. There was a slight whiff of stale lager and perfumed talc that's supposed to get rid of carpet smells. I pulled my old sleeping bag over me and turned over on the hard floor.
Gawd!
I came eyeball to eyeball with a red faced fellow smelling of whisky.
I think I'll move.

Around midnight there was an announcement over the Tannoy. We had arrived in Orkney.
Thanks for waking me up Captain, just as I was dropping off too.
After a while the engines started again and we were off. Next stop, Lerwick. I tossed and turned in rhythm with the waves. I noticed Rhys pop out and back again.
'Where have you been?'
'I went to the loo. It's horrible. There was a man vomiting into the hand basin and there was sick all over the toilet floor. Here, you better have one of these, just in case.' He thrust a pristine paper bag in my face.
Some comfort blanket.

'Rhys, are you awake? I think we're coming into land.' I said, a few hours later peering over him into the night. 'I can see a few lights.'

'Ooh, I'm stiff,' he winced, one eye opening. White stubble sprouted from his jaw. He looked like Jack Nicholson in 'As good as it gets.'

'Fancy a coffee?'

We packed up our things and made our way to the buffet restaurant. The corridors were packed.

'Where have all these people come from?'

'Looks like they had something we didn't.'

'Yes. Cabins.'

It was seven thirty am, dark and misty as we wobbled off the Hjaltland into the terminal in Lerwick and freezing arctic weather. The rain ran in horizontal stripes across the car window.

'Put on the windscreen wipers, Rhys.' 'I can't see a thing. Watch out! That woman in a parka to your right. You nearly ran her over.'

Rhys rubbed the windscreen with his sleeve.

'Oh God, she's coming over. An argument would be a great start to the Shetland experience.'

'Hello. Are you Mr and Mrs Daniel?' a pale face asked, peeping out from a drenched parka.

'Yes. I'm sorry, I nearly ran you over,' said Rhys meekly.

'Dunna worry aboot tha'. I'm Caroline, Mary Stephenson's daughter.'

'Mary Stephenson?'

'Your landlady. My mither sends her apologies. She's in Norfolk. She asked me to meet you.'

'How thoughtful,' I said leaning across Rhys to shake her hand.

'No problem. If you follow that blue pick-up I'll take you to Strand Loch. It'll take aboot ten minutes.'

'Thank you. That's great.'

Smiles all round then.

Caroline ran over to the pick-up and Rhys edged the car behind her and out of the terminal. We picked up speed but could see very little except the headlights of oncoming traffic.

'It's busy for seven thirty in the morning, isn't it?' Rhys said.

'I suppose people are going to pick up their family and friends off the ferry or going to work in Lerwick.' I rubbed the misted window and peered out into the gloom.

'Looks like peat bogs.'

'Mmm. Caroline's going fast. I better concentrate. Don't want to lose her.'

We followed the van through the countryside until we reached a sign post that said 'Gott.'

'Gott's with us so we'll be alright,' Rhys smirked.

Too early for bad jokes.

The blue pick-up turned right and a mile or so down the road indicated right again and we followed it into a cul-de-sac. The pick-up pulled up at the house at the end and Caroline jumped out.

'Well, this is it Janet. Our new home in the north. What do you think?'

I'm tired. I want a cup of tea.

I had rented the house from a list that the Shetland Health Board had sent me but accepted no responsibility for and without actually having seen it myself.

This is a bit like computer dating. The moment of truth.

'Interesting, Rhys, interesting.'

Caroline ran up the path and opened the door to the Norwegian style wooden bungalow. We pulled down the hoods of our anoraks and made a dash for it.

'Coom in, coom in,' Caroline said, as she tried to pull the door against the strong wind.

'What a pity. Such bad weather to welcome you to Shetland. Well anyway, welcome to Shetland.'

Caroline showed us into the living room. It was a small room dominated by a dark blue three piece suite, a large oak dining table and a walnut cabinet.

'Sit doon and I'll make us a cuppa.'

'Great- um- it's very cold Caroline,' I whinged.

'You'll need tokens for the meter but I have one here and we'll soon get the storage heaters on. While the kettle's boiling I'll show you how to put the gas on.'

Rhys followed Caroline out to the back of the bungalow. I sat shivering on the edge of an armchair and looked out of the large picture window. It was still dark but I could see the loch emerging from the mist and rain.

What are they doing?

'We can't open the propane gas valve,' Rhys said, water dripping off his stubble.

'Dunnae worry. I'll phone my mither.'

Isn't she in Norfolk?

Caroline went back into the kitchen and came back with two mugs of hot tea.

'O.K. I've rung my mither. She sends her regards and suggested I ring a plumber friend. I've done that and he'll be here within the hour. Would you like to see around the rest of the hoose?'

We followed the landlady's daughter into the master bedroom looking out into the cul-de-sac. There was a bed, a built in wardrobe and a chest of drawers.

These Shetlanders are stalwart. There's no heater.

Then into the second bedroom next door also overlooking the cul-de-sac. There were twin beds and a built in wardrobe. Opposite the master bedroom was a good size bathroom with shower over the bath and toilet.

'How does the shower work?' I asked.

'I'm not sure. I've never lived here. We'll ask the plumber,' Caroline replied.

Then back, into the light square kitchen overlooking a large grassy lawn, a country road and the loch. Opposite the front door, Caroline opened a cupboard door.

'The utility room.' she said. We squeezed in. She showed us the water heater. There was also a washing machine and a fridge-freezer. There was a good size window on the left, looking on to the lawns of the neighbours and up the country road to the main road which we had just driven down.

We returned to the living room and waited for the plumber. The metal letter box rattled in the wind as if some demented spirit was trying to grab our attention.

Put a sock in it.

Rhys must have read my mind and went into the kitchen grabbed a teacloth and jammed it in the offending hole.

'How long does it take for the heaters to warm up?' he asked.

'They're storage heaters so by tomorrow they'll be working well.'

Tomorrow! I'll have pneumonia by then.

'Are you cold? I'll bring you a mobile heater over.'

'Thank you. Where's the nearest shop by the way?' asked Rhys.

'About three miles west over the hill and you can buy electricity tokens there too,' Caroline said, pointing out through the picture window to a road rising beyond the loch. 'Or there's the Co-op in Lerwick, about five miles away. It has a bigger selection.'

So there'll be no just popping out for the odd pint of milk.

We sat making polite conversation for a while, when suddenly I heard,

'Helloo,' and a guy in orange overalls opened the door and walked into the hall.

Caroline introduced the plumber and he and Rhys went around the back to sort out the gas. They were back in a jiff.

'All done. You can user your cooker now. You just needed a bigger tool,' he smiled.
Mmm.

'Do you have everything you need? If so, I'll be off to work,' said Caroline.

'Thank you so much for meeting us and buying us some provisions. Can we reimburse you?' I asked.

'Heck, no. I'll pop the heater over later. Bye.'

'Right, shall we get this party started?' I asked Rhys, throwing my arms around his neck. 'Yubber yubber doo!'

The following day the weather was a bit brighter and from our picture window we could see a small air strip tucked in behind the loch and more clearly the road following peat and heather bog land to the Westside. We decided to do a sortie of Gott. In the cul-de-sac there were twelve houses, a row of light brown wooden bungalows like ours and a row of two story houses in the Norwegian style, alternating red, blue and green. Through a small gate next to our house was a large reddish building, Tingwall Public Hall and adjacent to that Tingwall Primary School. Although our address was Gott, it seemed that Tingwall embraced a larger area. After the school there were several large bungalows fringing the loch. Walking out of the cul-de-sac and turning left towards the main road, there were several more houses and we saw a sign for kennels and several Shetland ponies playing in the field. That was Gott.

The day after we noticed that that there was a farmers' market in Tingwall Public Hall. We bought homemade lemon curd, banana cake and lobster legs, and wandered around looking at local organic produce, arts & crafts.

'This might be a good place to try and sell your paintings,' I said to Rhys over a cup of tea.
'Yes, maybe, but I've got to paint some first. Also, we'd better take things a little slowly. They may think we're being pushy.'
We chatted to the women serving tea and cakes and asked about activities in the hall. We discovered that there had been Keep Fit and Art classes in the past, but now the hall was mainly used for youth club, dances, functions, and meetings of the Scottish Rural Women's Institute. I expressed vague interest.
'You would be very welcome to come along to our meetings,' an attractive young blonde woman said to me, scribbling a telephone number on a piece of serviette.

'Are you serious about the Women's Institute?' Rhys asked me, as we walked across the car park of the hall and through the back gate into our cul-de-sac.

'You hate that sort of thing. You wouldn't join our local W.I, when you came to Wales. Why now?'

'Well, you're right. Part of me thinks it would be a good way of meeting other women and part of me knows I would hate it. I can't bake, I can't make jam, I can't knit, I can't do any of those housewifely things. You'd be better at that.'

'I don't think I'd qualify, somehow,' he laughed.

'Hey, what do you think if I was to suggest running an art class in the hall?'

'Now, who's being pushy? Come on, let's go and introduce ourselves to the neighbours.'

We stopped a young woman passing our house from the farmers market with her two young children and introduced ourselves. She was friendly and invited us to call in, so encouraged by this we knocked on our next door neighbour's door but there was no reply so we tried the next house. A smart elderly woman dressed in a tartan box pleated skirt came to the door.

'Good Morning. I'm Janet and this is Rhys and we've just moved into the end house.'

She probably thinks I'm a Jehovah's Witness or I'm selling something.

'Nice to meet you,' she smiled. 'I'm Violet. I'll call my husband. Bobby!'

An elderly man limped to the door supported by a stick.

'These people have just moved into Mary's place.'

'Have you come for the trees?' Bobby asked with an amethyst twinkle in his eye. We all laughed. I explained about my job with the Shetland Health Board.

'I was a district nurse before retirement,' said Violet. 'I'm from Perth and Bobby's a Shetlander. Look, why don't you come in?'

'Thank you, but we won't today as we're just going round to introduce ourselves to folk in the street, but we'd love to some other time.'

'You'd be very welcome,' she said. 'Michael next door usually pops in to see us on Saturday mornings, but I see his car isn't there so he must be out on errands. Margaret on the other side is in. Buses to Lerwick stop outside her place so if you need to know the bus timetable, she's the one to ask.'

We knocked on Margaret's door. I did the same introductory spiel.

'I'm looking after my grandson so you'd better come in,' Margaret said. She left the door open and went back into the house. We followed her into a replica of our own place, except the furnishings were lighter.

'Sit doon, sit doon. Can I get you a cuppa?'

I explained who we were, that we wouldn't stop on this occasion but could she tell us the times of the

Lerwick buses. She tore off a piece of paper from a pad and scribbled down some notes.

'I'm a widow,' she said, and her eyes glazed over.

Looks like I could be starting work already.

'Did you understand any of her story?' Rhys asked, when we got outside.

'Not much, I must admit.'

How am I going to do my job if I can't understand what clients are saying?

We continued down the road and knocked on every door. Most people were out or had seen us coming.

On Monday, in a caffeine induced state of alert I waved goodbye to Rhys and set off for Lerwick. As I got to the T junction I saw a continuous stream of cars wending their way over from the Westside, joining those from the north on the main road, a multi-coloured caterpillar heading slowly south to the capital. Turning left, I dropped into the slipstream of traffic, passing through peat and bog countryside, a small wind farm, a sodden golf club, a small loch, an L bend and more peat and bog. Suddenly, I was looking down on a harbour, the sea and in the far distance an island, which I guessed from the map must be Bressay. I followed the traffic down the hill, past the power station, the ferry terminal, the Co-op, and turned right, left past the Gilbert Bain Hospital, finally arriving at my destination. Total rush hour journey time- 15minutes.

I parked the car at the back of the health centre overlooking the sea and the end of Bressay and walked into the reception. I sat down with patients waiting treatment and tried to imagine myself seeing clients there. A few moments later a young looking man probably in his late thirties, early forties, with an athletic build, slim and tall, with dark brown hair and pale eyes came bouncing in through the main door.

'Good Morning, Janet. How was your trip?'

'Hello, Calum. Memorable, I think the word is.'

I had met Calum Andrews at the interview in July and he had spent a day of his weekend taking me on a spin of the mainland to give me a flavour of Shetland. Calum was originally from Fife, had lived and worked on Shetland for the past thirteen years, first as a Baptist minister and latterly as a counsellor. This was his first job as a counselling team manager. The day of the interview sparkled with sunshine and optimism and by the end of it I was in no doubt that I wanted to come and work there.

'Were you on the Orkney ferry? It was a rough ride, wasn't it? I put my head down and slept all the way.'

More fortunate than me, eh Calum .

'Come on, the team are all looking forward to meeting you. We're based at Montfield hospital just up the road, but I'm afraid our office isn't quite ready.'

Montfield had been the main hospital in Shetland until the Gilbert Bain Hospital, opposite the health centre, was built in the 1950s. It was now used for the elderly infirm and was the base for some of the other therapies. We walked up the stairs to the first floor.

'This will be our office,' he said.

'Will that be your chair, Calum?'

'No, the Dentist's chair is going,' he laughed. 'The question is when? It's screwed into the floor. This room should have been ready three weeks ago. I need to get onto Estates. Come on let's go and find the team.'

Adjoining Montfield via an enclosed ramp was a new extension to the building that was used for staff training and development.

'Oh, there they are,' Calum said, pushing open the door into a large room.

'Hello everybody. This is Janet.'

Three women were seated in a semi circle and they all got up to introduce themselves and shook my hand. I took my seat and Calum started the meeting. Apart from Calum the team of counsellors consisted of Tracy, Gerrie and Emily. As Calum spoke I studied my new colleagues:

Tracy, was the Senior Counsellor, a twinkly Lancashire lass of about 40, who had lived in Shetland as a teenager. She looked an athletic sort and I later learnt she had a passion for hockey, football and in particular Bolton Wanderers. Tracy would also work in

Lerwick and in Levenwick, a community in the south of the mainland.

Gerrie, a tall slim dark haired Shetlander, in her forties, had lived in Shetland all her life and had worked as an independent counsellor before the establishment of the new service. She would continue to work part-time in communities on the Westside.

Emily, an enthusiastic English woman also in her forties had lived on the island of Unst with her family for the past fourteen years or so. She would work part-time on the island of Yell and in Hillside, a community in the north of the mainland.

Calum as well as being the counselling manager would have a caseload, working in Levenwick and would pick up clients from Fair Isle. They were an interesting group and I was looking forward to getting to know them better.

I was the only new girl to Shetland and I would be in Lerwick, Whalsay and Unst.

'Did you have a nice holiday, Calum ?' Tracy asked.

Holiday? I thought the service had just started.

'Estates can't say when we'll be in our room yet,' she said. 'I've been round to see them every day. Also, there's no progress on a room for us at Lerwick either but now you're back perhaps we'll see some action.'

'Thanks for holding the fort, Tracy. Perhaps the three of us can go over after lunch and see what's happening.'

No admin base and no room to counsel in. Sounds like a good beginning for a new service.

'We need to get our policies and admin in place. Referrals will be done electronically. I need to set up your laptop.'

'What admin support do we have?' I asked.

What was that look, Tracy?

'It's something I'm working on Janet. They're under great pressure at Lerwick and want us to be self-sufficient. We'll have a few hours a week, but I'm afraid we'll have to do the bulk of it ourselves.'

Ah ha. Janet, try not to be negative on your first day.

After the meeting we went into the small staff canteen and had lunch. After we had eaten and exchanged small talk Calum said,

'Come on, time to sort out the room in Lerwick. Emily and Gerrie can book you all in for IT training.'

I look forward to that.

Tracy and I followed Calum down the hill, across the road and back into the health centre. The building was on two floors, with primary care on the ground floor to the front of the building and mental health services and procurement on the lower floor facing the sea. Calum took us round and introduced me to various members of staff. The Practice Manager was on the sick and his deputy suggested a meeting with herself and one or two of the GPs to see how we could fit our service into unavailable space. In the meantime, the Deputy Practice Manager made it clear that

although she did not wish to be unhelpful her admin team were so stretched that they could not book our appointments, take cancellations or messages for us.
Well, I guess there are always teething problems with new services.

That evening when I arrived home, Rhys welcomed me with a hug. I could see he was eager to talk.

'How's your day been? I asked. How did you get on at the Job Centre?'

'Well, there isn't much in the way of work available at the moment. There's a cleaning job at the Ministry of Defence I picked up an application form for. Are you ready to eat? I've made a cottage pie.'

'Thanks, not quite yet. What about teaching?'

'My qualifications have to be assessed by the Scottish education system plus there's the usual child protection checks. I did apply before coming, but today I was told it could take 3 months.'
Great.

'Were they able to tell you the likelihood of getting supply teaching once that's been done?

'Yes, they think it quite likely. There's a shortage of teachers.'

'Well, this may be the opportunity to get on with your own art work. I'm not sure that the MOD would give you a job, what with your previous history of direct action and painting out English road signs. Or perhaps that could go in your favour in Scotland?'

'Yes, but that was a long time ago... How was your first day?'

'Well, there's a lot of politics going on. There's no available space for one of us let alone two to do counselling in Lerwick at present, and the admin base isn't ready yet. Oh, and we're going to have to do most of our own admin. So, I'm not sure how or where we're going to provide a service. Shall we eat?'

Most of the next couple of weeks was spent wandering around looking for space to work and trying to get to grips with the IT system, which didn't seem to interface too well with the one in Lerwick Health Centre. Calum, Tracy and I had several meetings with people from primary care and procurement. Finally, the secretary of one of the senior community nurses offered to give up her room on a temporary basis and she squashed into a small room with her boss. Difficult for the senior nurse but at least one of us was catered for. A complicated rota was designed, so that either Tracy or I would be peripatetic and use whichever doctor's room might be available for half a day at a time. Difficult for clients who like continuity and disruptive for us. The room was opposite the main reception area, so confidentiality was also a potential problem. Nobody wants to be seen visiting a counsellor. The room also needed sound proofing. Other than that, perfect.

It seemed that in recent years the infrastructure had not kept pace with the development of services across Shetland. There was also great pressure on room space in the health centres on the outer islands as most of the therapies, such as physiotherapy and podiatry were provided by visiting therapists, who had to compete for space with the GP, practice nurse, and community health visitor based there. In the second week, Calum suggested we visit my first outer island Whalsay, where I would be counselling on one day a fortnight. Whalsay (pronounced Walsa) or Whale island in Old Norse, is to the east of the mainland. It is about a forty minute drive from Lerwick to the ferry at Laxo.

'Come on, we better get going if we're going to catch the eleven o clock ferry,' Calum said, as he jumped into his little red car and Tracy and I tried not to be left behind.

Don't get in the way of the man with a mission.

We drove through the countryside at break neck speed and arrived at Laxo to see the large yellow ferry, called Bigga, pulling into the tiny harbour. After a quick turn around Calum drove on to Bigga.

'Just made it. Fancy a coffee?' he asked. 'You go on up and I'll sign the book. You need to sign on every outward journey.'

Tracy and I sipped our cappuccino in the luxury of a comfortable cabin with large picture windows and great views of the receding mainland and Whalsay in the distance.

I'm going to enjoy this bit of the job.

'How long does it take?' asked Tracy.

'About twenty minutes. Just in time for you to finish your coffee,' he laughed.

'Whalsay has a population of about 800 and more millionaires per square meter than anywhere else in Britain. The money comes from fishing,' Calum said, as we drove off the ferry and headed up the hill towards the health centre.

Millionaires? Well, from those few dreary pebble dash houses we've just passed you'd never have guessed.

We arrived at the health centre and Calum introduced me to the GP and the Practice Manager.

'Well, I don't know where we can put you,' the GP said. 'As you can see we're short on space and every room is used every day, that is except possibly the occasional Monday and Wednesday.

'Monday is the only day the whole team can meet because of pressures on rooms in other centres,' Calum said.

'Wednesday is one of the few times that there is a room in Lerwick,' Tracy piped up.

'The logistics of this gets complicated.' Calum muttered. Everyone shook their heads. Then Chrissy, the Practice Manager said,

'There is somewhere, but I'm not sure it would be suitable.'

She led us into a small corridor and pointed at the kitchenette, three metres by two, complete with centrifuge machine, drugs refrigerator, defibulator, sink and kettle, and just enough space for two chairs with toes touching. I had had clients before who tried to play psychological footsie with me but this degree of physical intimacy felt invasive.

You're too young to remember Dunkirk but check your upper lip to see if you can stiffen it.

'O.K. I'll give it a go. Would Tuesday be convenient?'

The following Tuesday I did the trip alone and got myself settled into my new counselling room. I put a 'Meeting in Progress' notice up on the door, a euphemism in counsellor speak for: 'Don't dare enter. Someone may be in tears, just disclosed something terrible from their childhood or be very angry. Stay out!'

'Sorry to interrupt,' a younger GP said, as he barged in on my first session.

'I need to use the centrifuge machine urgently,' he said leaning over me and inserting vials of blood into the machine. 'It makes quite a bit of noise I'm afraid.'

'What did you say?' I shouted at my client, who could have been speaking a foreign language for all I knew. As the glass vials of blood spun at the speed of light making the noise of a lawn mower in full throttle, she attempted to tell me her problem. Just thinking about blood makes me nauseous.

Concentrate. Don't think about the blood.

After much mouthing and gesticulating the machine suddenly stopped without warning and just at the point when she shouted at the top of her voice,
'My problem is that GP, who's just interrupted us. He's just not taking me seriously.'

At lunchtime I went out for a brief stroll. At first impression walking around Whalsay was like walking around a select council housing estate with pebble-dash houses built for the gales and untidy gardens, the product of them. Apparently they are like mansions inside, full of beautiful furniture and artefacts brought up from the south by container load. Shetland is one of John Lewis's biggest UK customers. I went back to face more clients. I was really struggling with understanding the dialect and squirming at my lack of local knowledge.

My next client was a young woman whose family had shares in a boat that often went up to Iceland and Norway to fish. In her story she mentioned that the Skipper was waiting to pack up.
'What fish was he wanting to pack up?' I asked, trying to remember if pelagic fishing meant mackerel, herring or cod.
'Pack up fish?
'Yes,' I said repeating what I'd heard her say.
'Pack (Pick) up the other fishermen,' she reiterated. We both started to laugh, something I am told is very good for people who come for bereavement

counselling.

Gott

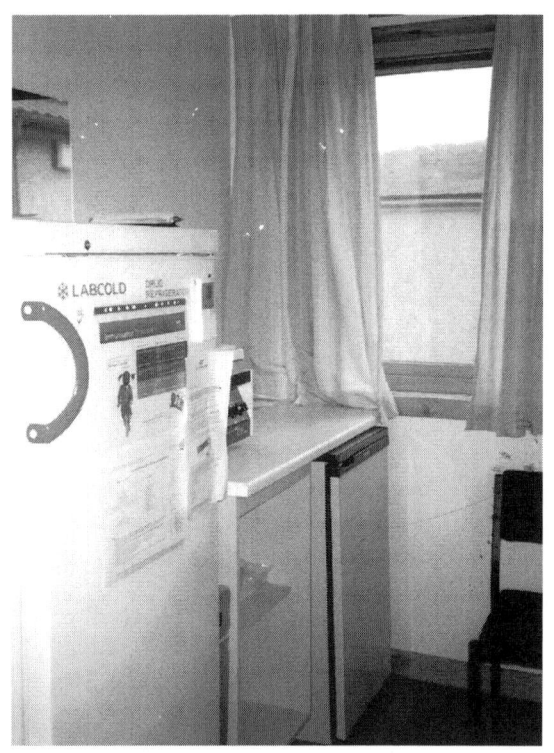

Counselling Room, Whalsay

November 2004

'Come and have a look at my studio,' Rhys said one evening just as I got through the door from work.
Do I have to right now?

It was becoming clear that after a day of seeing and speaking to no-one he was keen to engage me in conversation. Although I hadn't really started working at full stretch yet, after a day of listening and talking to people with problems it was the last thing I wanted to do, but if this arrangement was going to work for us I needed to be patient.

'Do I have to right now?' I whinged. 'I've just got in, I'm tired and hungry.'

He blushed.

'O.K. I'm sorry, come on show me.'

Rhys opened the door to the utility room. He had set up a drawing board over the fridge freezer, a small step ladder was his stool. On higher shelves over the washing machine he had placed his paints. There were boxes of charcoal and pastels. He'd put up some postcards and photos on the inside door and on door of the boiler. On the drawing board he had started a small picture.

You cow, you couldn't be as self-sufficient as this.

'How inventive. It's very small though. Wouldn't you prefer to use the back bedroom?'

'No, this has good light and I can see part of the loch and the windmills in the distance.'

'Isn't it cold, having your legs pressed against the freezer?'

'No, I tend to stand up and the boiler keeps the room quite warm. What do you think of my drawing?'

'Well, it's not tree roots, that makes a change, and a lot of colour. I like it. Unusual for you to do landscapes.'

'I thought I'd do some views from our window, the dawns and sunsets have been dramatic, with the idea of trying to sell some at the December farmers' market, that is if it's not too expensive to hire a stall.'

'Great idea. Any luck with the MOD application?'

'No, I haven't heard anything yet. By the way Violet popped in this morning.'

'Oh yes?'

'She wanted to know if you'd like to come to the next W.I. Meeting.'

'Hello Rachel, how are you?' I said, tucking my feet up on the armchair, getting cosy for our regular telephone call a few nights later.

'Alright,' she said unconvincingly.

'What's wrong?'

'I'm exhausted. I've prepared two lessons and have another three to do by tomorrow.'

'It's 10pm now. What time are you working to?'

'Midnight probably.'

'Is there anyone you could ask to help?'

'Not really.'

'Can I help?'
'Not really.'
'How are you finding the journey?'
'Great. Thirty miles each way. I go to school in the dark and come back in the dark. You know how I like night driving. Today, there was an odd noise coming from the engine.'
Oh shit.
'Do you want to speak to Dad about it?'
'Not really.'
'Perhaps you should take it to the garage.'
If Rhys was home he'd be sorting this out for you.
'It's closed by the time I get home.'
'Well, the weekend then. We'll pay. If you do break down you know you can ring the ETA breakdown service. How's the lodger?'
'She's in the next room.'
'So you can't talk then?'
'No.'
'Just answer yes or no.'
'O.K.'
'Is she helping with the cleaning?'
'No.'
'Do you share any meals.'
'No.'
'Do you see much of each other?'
'No.'
'Does she know anything about English teaching?

'You've got to be joking. Look Mum, thanks for calling, but I've got to get on with this preparation.'

'O.K. love. Sorry I can't help. I'll call you tomorrow.'

'Time to visit your next place of work,' Calum said a few days later.

My next island was Unst, the most northerly island in the British Isles. It was a bright day as Calum, Tracy, Emily and I set off on the journey. It felt a bit like a work's outing. Although just over a hundred odd miles away it would take at least two and a quarter hours if we made all the ferry connections. I would be making this return journey once a fortnight. We were soon out of Lerwick and into the treeless countryside.
No great oaks or beech here to wave you on your way.

The first part of the journey mirrored the one for the Whalsay ferry. The landscape soon emptied itself of people and gave way to slopes of peat, heather and pools of shiny water. We passed the odd grand Norwegian kit house perched on the edge of a small bay and roofless crofts with heavenly views of the sea and islands. Everywhere I looked was water; whipped up fresh water lochs, where you don't need a licence to fish for trout, and the North Sea and Atlantic Ocean playing hide and seek with us to right and left. At Voe, about fifteen miles from Lerwick we turned right and further north we went, up the winding road to Toft.

'Those abandoned stone cottages cast a sad shadow on the landscape. Why don't they do them up?' I asked.

If this was Wales, this would be a landscape of barn conversions.

'It's cheaper to build a new house on the site. You don't pay VAT.' Calum said.

'Ah yes, I see the new builds alongside the ruins of old family homes.'

Not far from Toft we passed the burnt-out remains of the oil workers' social club and cheap-build boxes to house them.

'In the eighties this was a boom town. These roads and much of Shetland's infrastructure is built on revenue from North Sea oil. The industry's heyday has passed and the houses you can see are now used for social housing,' Calum said driving fast, concentrating on the road ahead.

We arrived at Toft to catch our first roll-on roll-off ferry across Blue Mull Sound to Ulsta in south Yell, an island between the mainland and Unst. There was a long queue of cars.

'Oh heck, I didn't think we'd need to book,' Calum said.

What's that look, Emily?

'It looks like there's a funeral today,' she said.

Fortunately we did manage to squeeze the car on. As we stood on the deck, the mainland slipped away from us and silhouettes of small uninhabited islands scattered across the waters emerged like sleeping policeman.

'What kind of sailor are you?' asked Calum as he looked up at the sky. Grey lumps of cloud were forming.

'I'm not sure. I'm usually ok, but this is all new to me.'

'What about you?'

Calum waved his hand in a comme ci comme ça movement.

Not that good then.

The ferry was brand new, costing the Council a few million pounds.

'It was only in operation for a few weeks when there was an accident in getting it into its mooring,' Emily said. 'The Skipper was suspended and a petition is circulating to have him reinstated.

'What happened?' Tracy asked.

'He'd been given little training in this new hi-tech craft, the older craft was much smaller, easier and quicker to manoeuvre.'

To distract us, Emily went off and found the coffee machine and brought back steaming cappuccinos. Before we had finished our drinks and anecdotes about accidents at sea the ferry arrived safely at Yell.

We had twenty two minutes to drive from the south to the north of the island to catch the connecting ferry to Belmont in Unst. If we missed it we would have at least a half an hour to wait for the next one, making us late for our appointment with the GP. Calum put his foot down.

I'd like to arrive in one piece please but as you're my new boss I can't tell you that-yet. Stuff your hand in your mouth to stop yourself squealing, girl.

We zoomed along a straight clear road that could have been an aircraft run way. That is except for the sheep and as every Shetlander will tell you, sheep are stupid, but Yell sheep are the stupidest of all. Calum swerved to avoid the fluffy obstacles squatting on the warm tarmac or cruising across the road as if they were a family of Italians on a Sunday evening Volta.

'Missed it, damn! and there's no mobile contact. I hope Dr Hamish hasn't anything else on his agenda this afternoon,' said Calum .

Should have gone faster, eh?

'Never mind, we can have something to eat,' Emily said, pointing at the sign for 'The Wind Dog Café.' We made our way in and Emily introduced us to the owner, a young man wearing a hat with a fishy batik design.

'Michael is an opera singer,' she said with great deference, 'but unfortunately he's lost his voice today.' Michael held his throat and mouthed that the special was beef soup. We sat down as he took Emily to the back of the café to show her the fruit and veg patterned patchwork quilt squares he'd just got off of eBay. The café was full of knick-knacks in glass cabinets, the sort you'd find in a 1950's front room. There was a small library, art for sale and an internet connection. The walls of the toilets were painted with seaside scenes.

'Is he the only gay in the village?' I whispered as she sat down at the table.

Emily blushed.

Watch it, you don't want her to think you're not PC.

'He had quite a hard time when he first came here. Yell folk can be cautious about newcomers, but the café has brought business to the island. He is an active community artist, running singing groups and music workshops. He's well liked and now very well integrated into the island community.'

Not just the village then.

At that moment, Michael appeared with the soup. Calum was still looking pale from the ferry and obstacle race.

What is that?

I looked down at the thick sticky black mixture with unmentionable bits of animal floating on top and made a mental note to have something else from the menu next time.

Stick to the singing, Michael.

'Looks like the ferry is about to go,' Emily said, and we made our way back to the car. The ferry across the Sound was a much smaller and older one, also calling at the smaller island of Fetlar to the east of Yell. There was no cappuccino machine on board so we sat in the car and looked at the car bumper ahead through a curtain of light drizzle.

The Unst Health Centre was a fifteen minute drive from the ferry. The island flashed by.

'Well, this is a surprise! What do we owe the honour, Calum?' Joan, the smiley receptionist asked.

'Weren't you expecting us? We have an appointment with Dr Hamish and we're late'

'Oh, he didn't say anything. Hold on, I'll go and see if he's around.'

Around? Don't say we've come all this way for nothing.

A few minutes went by and Dr Hamish appeared looking like a Yell sheep.

'I thought you were coming next week,' he said, flushing. He ushered us into his consulting room and explained that there was really nowhere in the health centre for me to see clients as each room was in use every day, either by his own staff or visiting therapists.

'Is there a kitchen? I asked.

Call me the Kitchen Counsellor, the therapeutic equivalent to Jamie Oliver.

'There is, but that's used by the Practice nurse, when the Physio uses her room.'

'What about using a room up on the air base, five miles further north at RAF Saxavord?' he asked.

As we drove along the straight open road of empty countryside past derelict crofts and small RAF housing clusters we fell silent. Unst felt like another country in another time zone with an advanced weather system. A bit like a black and white *John le Carré* film set in the eastern bloc during the cold war. Quiet shouted at me in a loud voice.

Oh shit, what have I done? Why did I accept this post? What am I doing here?

My heart slipped into a black hole and whizzed round like a lost star shedding its light. I felt my colleagues' gaze. I swallowed hard.

What's wrong with you, you wimp? You've done Voluntary Service Overseas in Indonesia. You can do hard. I don't want to. What is this all about?

RAF Saxavord controlled Britain's early warning radar system in case of attack from northern enemies or aliens. 'Bikini Black Alert' must have meant we posed no danger as there was nobody in uniform to welcome or bar us from entry.

They can't be expecting an attack from within then.

We drove past the medical centre.

Surprise, it's shut.

We noticed the NAAFI, the most northerly Spar in Britain, but decided to give it a miss.

'Cheer up. I live here!' said Emily.

You work here then.

'Confidentiality is a huge issue on a small island,' she said.

Yes, but it's going to take me five hours to get here and back.

'Although Emily has worked as an independent counsellor here for a few years with great success, she requested a change,' Calum said.

'I think the islanders will welcome an outsider,' Emily added enthusiastically.
Oh yeh.
'Tracy, you're quiet. What do you think?' I asked as we strolled around in the mist.
'I'm glad it's not me working 'ere,' she grinned, as she put her arm around me and gave me a squeeze.
Well, thanks a bunch Tracy.
Emily called over,
'Come on, I'll show you Bobby's bus shelter.'
We got back in the car and drove south towards Baltasound. In the back of the car I texted Rachel from my mobile.
Ooh, a signal.
'On way back from nowhere.'
'What's nowhere like?' she responded.
'Nowhere is foreign.'

The bus shelter in the middle of nowhere had been her son's idea and won him a Yahoo website of the year award, but I believe that it was Emily's sense of the surreal that had made this a Shetland landmark on the tourist trail. In an ordinary plastic bus shelter, decked out with lace curtains and a carpet, you can sit in an armchair, watch an unplugged TV, play imaginary computer games, make toast in the unplugged toaster, speak to the stuffed giraffe, all while waiting for a bus that rarely comes.
'I love it, Emily,' I said. 'This installation deserves a place in the Tate Modern.'

As we drove away Emily pointed to an amoebic shape in front of the bus shelter.

'That is going to be the John Peel Memorial Roundabout,' she said. 'We're planting potatoes on it next week.'

Not teenage kicks, but I think John would have appreciated the sentiment.

'Hi Liam, how are you doing?' I asked my son on the phone a few days later.

'We haven't heard from you for a little while. How's Uni?'

'Err... It's alright, but'

'Yes?'

'I'm not too sure about the course.'

'What's the problem?'

'It's all maths. It's boring.'

'And the people on the course?'

'They're all geeks.'

'You mean they like maths?'

I could hear my son smile.

'Well, I guess it's early days yet. It's bound to take time to settle in.'

'Yes, but it's been over a month now. Some of the guys are really into their courses.'

'Oh dear, I wish I could be there to help.'

'You can't really help, Mum.'

'Look, maybe it would be a good idea to go and talk to someone, your tutor for instance.'

'Nah. I don't like the guy.'

'What about seeing how it goes until Christmas? At the same time check out other possible courses and what the procedure for changing is. You got good A level grades in art and geography. What about going to see someone in those departments?'

'Yeh, maybe. Oh, Mum,'

'Yes Liam?'

'I've got a little beauty on my chin.'

'Well, don't pick it! Eat more greens.'

We both laughed.

'Look, I'll call you in a few days to see how you've got on.'

Shit.

'The umbilical cord couldn't stretch that far,' Calum said the following Monday, as we sat in our freshly renovated office base at Montfield ready to start the team meeting.

What are you on about, Calum?

'It was a big thing for you to come to Shetland leaving your family and friends and then I asked you to go a step further away from the mother ship. I experienced that to some degree when I left Fife to take up my ministry here thirteen years ago, but I had my children with me.' His pale eyes welled up.

What are you crying for? It's me that's got to work there.

'As a child did you ever feel abandoned?' he asked and set out his psychological theory as to why I might have been so affected by our visit to Unst.

'Let's see how we can get around this,' he said and we proceeded to discuss ways in which the mother ship could take more of the strain.

'What about in the winter months to save you having to do most of the trip in the dark, subject to the GPs agreement of course, you see Unst clients in the surgery in Yell. They're a nice bunch there. That would mean clients having to get a ferry, but it might overcome some of the problems folk have over confidentiality.'

'Yes, I could also offer telephone and video counselling to those unable to travel.'

'Fine. We will review the situation in the spring. *What a boss! I could hug you Calum, but you might get the wrong idea.*

As the month went on we started to receive invitations. Emily invited us over for lunch one Sunday, where we met her Scottish husband Donald, a committed community economic development worker, Bobby, of the bus shelter and their delightful little daughter. The couple had worked in the Sudan, Ethiopia and Nepal before coming to Shetland and there were interesting photos and artefacts lining their walls. A piano dominated the living room with a selection of shiny guitars standing upright ready for action. It seemed they were part of an active and creative community in Unst. The house was warm and cosy, smelling of home baking and close family.

You have a family, Janet. You chose to leave it behind. Now get a grip and enjoy your dinner.

'This lamb is absolutely delicious, Emily. Is it local?'

'Yes, I have a little man.'

Are there lepracorns on Unst?

'A little man?'

'Don't breathe a word.'

'Sorry?'

'Let's say, there's no butcher on Unst,' Donald intervened.

'Oh? The children are visiting in the new year. They would adore to eat lamb like this, do you think the little man might help?'

'I can't promise, but I'll see what I can do,' Emily winked.

'Do you know about the film club?' Gerrie, the counsellor from the Westside asked one Monday mid-morning as we wandered into the Montfield canteen for our coffee break.

'Yes, I noticed an advert in the Shetland Times.'

'It's art house films. You can either pay a yearly sub to be a member or pay at the door. It's fortnightly throughout the winter at the North Atlantic Fisheries College in Scalloway'

'Is there a cinema in Lerwick?'

'There's the Garrison Theatre that shows commercial films over a weekend once a month.'

Once a month? We're used to going to the cinema every week.

'I wondered if you'd like to come with Joe and I this week? You can eat at the Fisheries College, but we usually go for fish and chips in Scalloway after work and then onto the film. Would you like to join us?'
'That would be lovely Gerrie, thank you.'

That Thursday evening we set off for Scalloway (pronounced Scallowa). There was a gale force 8 raging and our car rocked as we drove on the narrow back road via Tingwall Loch to the College some five miles south-west of the Strand. This village was the original capital of Shetland, and the place from which the Shetland Bus did its sorties to and from Norway on behalf of the Resistance in World War 2, picking up partisans and dropping off equipment. These were dangerous expeditions in small boats, where brave Shetland and Norwegian men put their own lives on the line in the interests of the war effort against the Nazis. As a result there has been a close relationship of mutual respect and affection between the two that persists even until today.

'Hello, you made it,' said Gerrie laughing as we took off our dripping anoraks and sat down in the back of the Chinese fish and chip shop.

'You may want to keep those on, it's freezing,' she said.

'This is Joe.'

Joe got up and Rhys and I lent over the small table, shook his hand and introduced ourselves. A round friendly bespectacled face smiled back.

My God, it's my cousin Alex. What's he doing in Shetland?

'Are you related to the Teal family in Stepney, Joe?'

'Not that I am aware,' he laughed.

Pity.

We exchanged pleasantries and brief histories. I noticed Gerrie was on nodding or speaking terms with everyone who came into the café.

I wonder if it will ever be like that for us?

Joe told us that he was English and had been in Shetland for over twenty years. He had come to Shetland as a journalist and photographer and worked on the Shetland Times newspaper for many years. He now worked part-time in IT support at Shetland Health Council and part-time in environmental research, specializing in nuclear issues for the Shetland Islands Council.

'So you know who to blame when the IT system isn't working,' Gerrie teased.

'It's the NHS systems, not us,' he replied. 'Come on, better get going,' Joe said. 'The film starts in ten minutes.'

'Pity about the sound,' Gerrie said, as we came out of the College a couple of hours later. 'There isn't usually a problem.'

Just our luck.

A month or so before coming to Shetland I was chatting to one of my colleagues at Gwent Family Mediation, who told me she had a married brother, Bob, living in Shetland. She offered to write and give him and his wife Maggie our details.

'Maggie is particularly sociable. My mother has been to some great parties up there. I'm sure they'll invite you over,' she said.

Just before coming we received a lovely letter from Maggie urging us to get in touch once we were settled.

'Who was that?' Rhys asked, as I got off the phone one evening.

'Maggie. Her and Bob have invited us out for dinner at a restaurant near where they live.'

'That's nice. People are making a lot of effort for us, aren't they?' he said, looking over the top of his reading glasses.

'Well, some people are. The GPs haven't made a bit of effort. I'm particularly annoyed with the Welsh speaking GP. It's not like there are many other Welsh speakers here.'

'I suppose people have their own busy lives and families.'

Still think he could have done better.

That weekend we made our way to Brae, a community north of Voe and on to Busta, and the restaurant. As we entered the bar a small sparkly woman with spiky blonde hair waved and beckoned us over. Maggie introduced herself. A handsome tall and well-built man stood up and gave us both a firm handshake and introduced himself as Bob. Maggie is a Shetlander and she and Bob had lived in Cornwall for many years, while Bob was working and travelling with the Royal Navy. They had come back to live in Shetland several years ago when an opportunity arose for Bob to get a civilian job at Sullom Voe, the oil terminal. Unfortunately, in the last year he had had health problems leading to early retirement and the couple now focused on life on their croft rearing sheep. Maggie also worked as a home help.

'You'll have to come over and see our place,' said Maggie at the end of a pleasant evening.

'We'd love to. Thank you.'

'They've sorted out the room,' Tracy called, leaning on the reception desk at the entrance of Lerwick Health Centre as I waltzed in feeling buoyant after a good weekend.

'Thank God for that, it's only taken them two months.'

Tracy came from Lancashire, but had family in Shetland and had lived there for a few years as a teenager. Things hadn't worked out for her in nurse training and she returned to the British mainland vowing she would return to work and live in Shetland at some time in the future. Her career had been interesting. She had been a traffic warden, a police woman and now as a qualified and experienced counsellor she had returned to show Shetland what she could do second time around.

Tracy opened the door of a small room and I noticed she'd already made it her own, with her Bolton Wanderers posters and a cuddly tiger toy.

Looks like a teenager's bedroom. I'll just have to put them away when I'm counselling.

'Is this the way to Amarillo? There's a girl who's waiting for me.' I hummed the team's anthem as I pictured Tracy and I on the treadmill, like Parkinson and Ronnie Corbett on the TV.

Which one of us will fall off first?

'What are the referrals like?' I asked.

'Pretty good. There's about twenty here for starters, but once the doctors know we're fully operational I'm sure the floodgates will open. Here, have half!' she said thrusting a wodge of papers into my hand.

'Watch it Tiger! What happened to the electronic referral system?'

'It seems that a few of the Doctors aren't too comfortable with it.'

We're all having to make adjustments.

'Is that the Art Therapist?' I asked, when a broad Whalsay accent greeted me at the other end of the line. I had been thinking about my first visit to Unst and the overwhelming feeling of desolation and alienation I had experienced that seemed out of proportion to the situation. Perhaps Calum was right,

maybe it was something from my childhood and that exploring it with a therapist would help me during this transition period. It is not unusual for therapists to have therapy, in fact it is usually a compulsory component of training. How can you expect your clients to tell you their inner most secrets if you have never experienced what that's like? It builds self-awareness, brings the unconscious into the conscious, and is supposed to make you a more effective counsellor.
So they say.

A few days later I made my way up Lerwick's Commercial Street. The sky was splashed with rose like a watercolour painting. I filled my lungs with cold fishy air bracing myself for my first ever session of art therapy.

As I nervously entered her studio from one of the town's steep and windy lanes, my first impression of Freya, the art therapist, was of Valkyre. Her sculptured features, green-grey eyes and mop of blond hair gave her the look of a Viking warrior woman. She gave me a warm friendly grin and said something I couldn't understand.
This is going to be an interesting cultural experience.

She pointed to the kettle. As she went to put the coffee on, I sat on the wine coloured sofa in front of a large painting of a roaring fire and looked around at the child like paintings on the walls, tins of coloured paint and paper overflowing from the shelves. So different from Rhys's poky utility room studio. I felt excited at the thought of being creative and apprehensive at the thought of therapy.

'Shall I put the fire on?' she asked.

What a great way to start. She's guessed my appetite for the surreal.

Then she went to the back of the studio and put on the convector heater.

'Now, tell me about yourself.'

Freya sat in one of the big armchairs with her Viking head tilted and her palms open on her lap as if she were about to do a yoga exercise. She listened and listened as I droned on about myself, what I was doing in Shetland, how I'd reacted in Unst, how I was missing my children, and on and on.

I wish I could listen with such rapt attention without interrupting my clients. She's O.K.

'Do you want to draw your feelings?'

'I warn you, I'm a hopeless draw-er.'

'You don't have to be able to draw in order to do art therapy. In fact in some ways it helps if you don't. Many people revert to child-like marks on the page.'

'That makes me feel a lot better,' I said eager to take up a brush.

Freya poured thick creamy primary colours into a small pallet and I drew circles and lines.

'Ooh, that's interesting,' she said

Well Freya dear, if you can make sense of this rubbish you're a better therapist than me.

'Do you want to talk about your painting?'

'I'll try, but I'm not very good at feelings.'

I poured out the details of an incident that had had happened some fifty-five years ago. It had been an accident at birth. In delivering me, the doctor had dislocated my hip. In those days it was not automatically checked after birth. It wasn't until I had passed my first birthday and was slow to walk that my mother noticed that as I crawled across the kitchen floor I was dragging one leg behind me. I would have to have a plaster put on under anaesthetic. This would encase my pelvis and hips pulling my legs apart as if I was frozen in some trapeze act that had gone horribly wrong. The plaster would have to stay on for a few months.

My parents took me into the children's ward for the operation and settled me into a cot with metal bars too high for me to fall out or escape. Through the distant porthole window of the ward I watched my smiling parents leave. I recalled the white starched face of the nurse in her round national health spectacles berating me for crying. I was eighteen months old.

'How did you feel when your parents left you with the nurse?' asked Freya.

'I was so scared I shit all over the crisp white sheets.'

'And what else did you feel?' she asked.

'I felt abandoned,' I replied, and felt a lump in my throat the consistency and size of a golf ball.

After the session I walked up the lane towards the health centre, noticing the different shades of grey, green, mauve and blue flagstones paving my way and pondering on my experience.

'You agreed we'd do *what* tonight?' Rhys leant forward not hearing, except I knew on this occasion he had heard very well. We had been here before because Rhys does not do dancing and I do. That is to say I would if I could and if I had a willing male partner. I have tried ballroom and salsa with women friends but I usually get to lead so I get confused when I dance with a man We had tried a jive class in Cardiff, but Rhys didn't like being picked on to dance with the teacher. I didn't understand why as she was a tall slim Polish girl with rhythm, but he said he couldn't take the public scrutiny. Anyway, he believed that standing so close to the blaring tape machine was the reason he had lost his hearing in the first place.

It was a long wet and windy drive to Walls (pronounced Waas), nineteen miles of single track road out on the west side of rural Shetland. Gerrie, my colleague had invited us in response to my enthusiastic inquiries about Shetland dancing.

'Come on, let's run for it,' I said battening myself down against the prevailing south-westerly coming straight off the Atlantic. Rhys's head disappeared into the gloom of his duffle coat. Inside the village hall some local people were standing around in their Fair Isle knitwear waiting for the action to begin.

'You'll soon warm up,' said a pale looking woman with narrow eyes.

'I bet she's the teacher,' said Rhys, looking nervous. 'Can we go now?'

The fiddler removed his gloves and started to tune up.

'Oh, give it a chance. We can't go until we've tried a couple of dances and not before Gerrie and Joe have arrived.'

'It's a two step- perfect for beginners.' I heard a familiar voice and looking around saw Gerrie and Joe coming towards us. Joe grabbed me and Gerrie pulled Rhys onto the dance floor.

'Nicely pointed toes,' admired Joe. My toes beamed at the compliment and sharpened into a winkle picker. We progressed on to waltzes and reels. The fiddler played faster and we darted about, up and down, backwards and forwards. Joe was a good dancer and I was having fun.

'Watch your dosey-does!' the teacher cried.

I looked over to Gerrie and Rhys. They looked as if they had become one, completely tied up in each other's arms, except their arms were knotted behind their backs and around their heads, looking like some multi-limbed two headed monster. The dance was in complete disarray. The teacher looked bemused and everyone else seemed to find it hilarious.

Another soothmoother who can't dance.

Those of us who had arrived in Shetland through the south mouth of the Sound were all referred to as southmouthers or soothmoothers in local dialect; that included not only the English, Welsh and Irish, but the entire Scottish population, as Shetland is as far north as you can get and still remain in the British Isles.

'It must be awful difficult for Rhys,' said Gerrie kindly, as we stood with our cups of tea in the break.

'What do you mean?'

'With his hearing and all.'

'Ah, his hearing, yes'

His hearing! You don't need good hearing to do folk dancing, you just need to follow the person in front of you and concentrate.

Then I took a glance over in his direction. He looked red faced and embarrassed. *Despite hating it, he's doing this for you. You should be grateful. Many men wouldn't even give it a go. You should be proud of him not irritated, you bitch.*

'Shall we sit the next one out, Rhys?" I asked, squeezing his hand. He smiled thankfully.

'Maybe you'd find the beginners' class easier and nearer to home.' the teacher said helpfully at the end of the evening. 'Most of the folk here have been coming for years.'

'I'm afraid I have some bad news,' said Tracy later on that week. 'Well, it's good news for me, but not for the service.'

'What's up? Don't tell me, you've been signed up for Bolton Wanderers.'

'I wish. No, I have an appointment down south for my foot operation.'

We've only just got started. Go on, leave me to slug it out alone in Lerwick Health Centre.

'Well, that's great news. You have been waiting a long time, haven't you?'

'Yes, but it means you'll have to slug it out alone in Lerwick.'

'Don't worry, I'll manage. How long will you be away?'

'Six weeks maybe.'

Let's say three months.

'When you off?'

'Not sure yet.'

'I can't believe Liam's twenty today,' said Rhys coming off the phone from wishing him a happy birthday.

'I know. I think of it as my birthday too.'

'Yes, and I've the birth injury to prove it,' he laughed, rubbing his knee.

'It's sad not being with him to celebrate, isn't it?'

'Yes, but he's celebrating with his friends.'

And I'm his pathetic mother who still thinks of him as eight years old.

Janet in her living room

Rhys in the kitchen

December 2004

'The Bonhoga has agreed to give me an exhibition,' Rhys regaled me at the door as I arrived home from Lerwick Health Centre a couple of weeks later.

'Hold on, let me get out of the wind," I said, still not having completely left the day's set of client personalities and their problems behind me. I could always tell when he hadn't seen anyone that day. He was at the door like a faithful labrador, ready to lick his mistress with pleasure at her homecoming and in anticipation of a decent dinner. Only Rhys invariably had prepared *my* dinner, no dog's dinner, but a feast of local fish and imported treats from the Co-op.

The Bonhoga was one of the best galleries in Shetland and to get an exhibition so soon after arriving was quite an accomplishment.

'It's a travelling exhibition. It won't actually be at the Bonhoga. It will start off at the exhibition space at the airport.'

'Don't tell me, and will travel by plane from there?'

'Well no, by car probably, but around some of the islands, Unst, Whalsay, Yell, as well as the Peerie Café in Lerwick.'

The Peerie (Small) Café was in the centre of town, served good food and was well frequented by tourists looking for original souvenirs.

Rhys had agreement to do an artistic study of Shetland's archaeological treasures, focusing on the remains of the Viking sites and settlements scattered across the islands, many over 2000 years old. At home, he had done a number of studies of monoliths and Celtic burial chambers. He was hoping to explore the visual and historical links between Shetland and Wales around the same period. However, his strength and reputation was built on his relationship with the Welsh landscape and his deeply felt connection with her trees, their roots and her geology. He felt rooted in Wales. This new project and relationship with a treeless landscape would present quite a challenge.

'I've also heard from the Education Department. It will take a few months to process my application for teaching supply.

That's a minus on the money front.

'But it will mean you can really focus on the project. When does the exhibition start?'

'In March 2005 and will circulate to community venues until the end of the year.'

'You'd better get cracking then!'

'Suppose I had,' he said, his aquamarine eyes sparkling.

'Well, that is fantastic news. Let's celebrate. Come here, Mr Pushy,' I said, pulling him close and engaging in a middle age snog.

Not quite the same as when you're twenty but still pretty nice.

We began to get into a routine. On the day that I worked on an outer island Rhys would accompany me and spend the day visiting sites of interest, sketching and taking photographs. On other days, while I was working in Lerwick he would use this source material to develop his paintings in his studio, cooped up in the warmth of Radio 2 and on the look-out for birds foraging around Strand Loch. It was a pity that we had arrived at the end of the migratory season but there were still lapwings and oystercatchers to appreciate. However, it was dark by three thirty and the weather was deteriorating. After work we did little except read, chat, listen to music, watch TV and go to bed early. We didn't fancy the smoky atmosphere of Lerwick's bars, some with live folk music. Rhys's hearing problem meant that he suffered loud music although I enjoyed it. However, we both loved the gentle peace of Strand Loch. Weekends were the best when we would go off to an undiscovered place, walk and enjoy the wildlife, the tranquillity and the landscape.

There were two shops in Shetland. Well, that's not quite true, there were other smaller shops, but only two big food shops in Lerwick. Not big by UK mainland standards of course, but called supermarkets none the less. The Co-op and Somerfield were situated at either end of town, so whether you were going north or south you would pass one of them. You'd be wise to stop and think carefully if there was anything you might need as the next time you might see a shop open could be on your way back from your trip and it would be the same shop.

One Friday evening on the way home from work, I stopped at the Co-op. I had just got out of the car, holding my umbrella close to my head as I ran for the entrance.

'Hello, Janet.' It was Calum coming out with his weekend ration of full-bodied red wine. I hardly recognised him with his anorak hood tied tightly under his chin and his pale eyes barely visible under his rain splattered spectacles.

'Those are two things you really don't need in Shetland,' he laughed.

'What's that Calum?'

'That crook-lock on your steering wheel. Shetland has one of the lowest crime rates in Britain and if it was stolen they would have nowhere to go. They'd be caught at the ferry.'

'Oh, right,'
I've given myself away yet again as an ignorant soothmoother.

'What's the second?'

As he pointed at my white umbrella a sharp draught of wind caught hold of it and whipped it out of my hand. We watched it lift, circle and dive like a gannet into the slushing water by the harbour wall.

'They say it will be a Force 10 tonight. 12 is a hurricane. A cosy night in, I think. You had better stock up.'

Every night is a cosy night in for us, Calum.

'In that case, I may have to call in at Chris Hodges, 'Bargains for all' and buy myself a parka for our weekend walk.'

'They are selling off their summer range. There's a patio heater going for £50.'

It's comforting to know I'll be warm on the patio in a Force 10, Calum.

Then I went into the Co-op and bought three cans of hairspray just in case we got a last minute invitation out.

'I haven't really seen Lerwick properly yet,' I said to Rhys the following morning. The gale had passed and white galleons floated across our lounge picture window sky. It was cold, windy but dry.

'I guess you've seen much more than me when you've been out with your portfolio. You can show me around.'

'Fine. We could have fish and chips at the Fort Café and pick up a DVD from the Toll Clock.'

We drove into town and parked in a small car park behind Commercial Street. There was a Saturday buzz about the place. Folks from the countryside strolling along; the middle aged in single file, the women checking out the latest fashions, the men behind them diverted by electrical goods; groups of teenagers hanging around the music shop; the odd tourist with camera and guidebook looking for somewhere good to have coffee.

'Let's go in here,' I said to Rhys pointing at Oxfam. 'I see they've got a big selection of books and.is that a Fair Isle pullover on the rack?'

A brand new sweater would cost around £80 to £100.

'Here, try this on,' I said, thrusting a 1970s sleeveless red and yellow pull-over in his hand. He pulled off several layers of clothing and put in on.

'Perfect. It will help you fit in to the Shetland dancing scene.'
What's that look?

We carried on walking up and then down the gently flowing main street, past bakery, butcher, electrical shop, various clothes and jewellery shops, music store, hairdresser, flower shop, newsagent, chemist, a fancy dress shop, a photographer, a couple of bars, craft shops, a fast food outlet, cafés, bank and estate agents until we reached the town square known as The Cross.

'It's nice that there are no big chain stores. Each shop is individual. I love the sandstone and the odd fluted mock tower. It's charming, isn't it Rhys?'

At The Cross, to the left was a small harbour and on the right the Tourist Office, a drop in service for young people and Shetland Soap, a commercial venture which supports people with disabilities in employment.

'This reminds me of Vision 2,' Rhys said. We had both worked with people with disabilities in our time and Vision 21 was a cutting edge service in Cardiff.

'I read that Shetlanders are extremely generous givers to good causes,' he said. 'The average for individual giving in England is something like 53pence a year, in Scotland 67pence and in Shetland £2.42p.'

'No cause too big or too small, eh? According to the Shetland Times, from the displaced in Iraq to a disabled toilet for the British Legion.'

'Up The Lanes,' he pointed to the right, 'is Hill Head, with the library, museum and town hall. The architecture is mainly Victorian.'

'Oh yes, and further back is Montfield.'

'Come on, let's cross the road, and have a look at the Lodberries,' he said grabbing my hand and avoiding a car at the bend in the road. We passed the R.N.L.I, housed in the renovated Old Tollbooth building, a few knitting and yarn, and art and craft shops. Then, along by the sea wall overlooking Bressay Isle we came on some old stone cottages.

'These are the Lodberries. In olden days boats would have delivered their goods straight to the back door and be winched up straight out of the boat into the store room.'

'They're lovely. Stop, let me take a photo.'

'Then if you carry straight on, you'll reach the Anderson High School. I think it's a legacy of the man who started P&O, the shipping company.'

'You have been doing your homework. I'm well impressed. Husband, I think you deserve your lunch.'

After lunch at the Fort Charlotte Cafe we drove to a small shopping mall, near the Co-op, the Toll Clock Shopping Centre, with more small shops, a video and DVD rental shop, and a travel agent with deals to exotic places at exuberant prices. Getting anywhere from Shetland is very expensive and time consuming. You have to get to the UK mainland first.

'Do you think McNabs will be open?' I said, as we got back in the car and headed for home. Gerrie, who in her time had been a chef, had recommended McNabs, a fish shop run by an elderly woman, who had worked as a herring girl. Until the early 1960s local girls followed the herring catch from Shetland to Grimsby, cleaning and salting fish straight off the boats, moving on by land as the boats went out to fish in the North Sea and land their catches further down the British coastline. What an adventure! Now her freezer offered a cornucopia of fresh varieties: salmon, fresh and smoked, clams, scallops, oysters, haddock, piltock, mackerel and many more. I had set myself a project; to try the lot.

There was another shop with a fishing connection which I preferred to visit without Rhys; a lingerie shop apparently also much frequented by local men. As time went on I was never sure if it was for themselves or their partners, as at local festivals many Shetland men seemed to enjoy dressing up as women.

Freya told me that one of the most popular shops with local fishermen was Ann Summers in Aberdeen. They bought up underwear and sundries by the crate load.

Every Friday we scanned the pages of the Shetland Times looking at houses and procrastinating about whether to buy or not to buy. At the weekend we would combine our sightseeing with visiting prospective homes, old dilapidated crofts or spanking new kit homes in remote places with spectacular views. The prices were low compared to home. In 2004 you could buy a beautiful three bedroomed kit house for around £130,000.

'We have to be sure we are going to stay,' said Rhys as we laid in bed late one Saturday morning deciding how to spend the day.

'We could always rent it out if we don't.'

'Yes, but how are we going to raise the deposit? Wouldn't it mean selling our home in Wales?' He raised himself onto his elbow and turned towards me to hear better.

'Bob advised not to sell up down south, because if you want to go back, you'll never be able to afford to get back on the property ladder.'

'Are we sure we're here for good? What about the children?' Rhys started to pull the skin under his chin.

'They'll be off themselves soon.' I started to get out of bed and pulled on my dressing gown.

'I'm not sure.'

'But I hate paying rent. We're paying £475 for this place plus £100 Council tax. It seems such a waste, when we could be spending the same amount for a place we will end up owning.'

'If in doubt..?'

' ...don't! I know. I am impulsive but it usually works, doesn't it? Remember that day I was feeling depressed and went out and bought a caravan?'

'Yes, most women when they are down would buy themselves a new dress. It was a surprise, and we've had lots of fun in it over the years.'

'Yes, but?'

'I like that side of you, it can be exciting; like when you broke the news that you'd applied for the job in Shetland. That was an initial shock.'

I'm the risk taker in this relationship, aren't I?

'I'm not very good at consulting first, am I?'

'Well, no, but buying a house on a remote island miles from home is a bit different to buying a second hand touring caravan, wouldn't you agree?'

Err, no.

'Did I tell you that I almost bought a house on Burra when I came up for interview? Are you O.K, Rhys? You've gone white.'

The days rolled on. Referrals for counselling at the health centre in Lerwick kept coming as Tracy had predicted; like a tsunami out in the Atlantic we feared they might soon overwhelm us. Reluctantly we had to start a waiting list. We were seeing clients, who in a UK mainland context may have been referred to psychology services, but with the lack of appropriate resources we were taking on complex cases. Clients' issues included bereavement, relationship and family difficulties, drinking problems, self-harm, sexual and emotional abuse, eating disorders, chronic anxiety, social phobia, and depression. Although I found this heavy at times, it was also challenging and interesting. I felt privileged as an outsider to have a unique insight into another layer of Shetland society and hopefully be able to offer some support to my clients. The waiting list meant we were able to have a manageable caseload and focus on the needs of our current clients.

However, Tracy and I worried about those whose needs we were not yet aware of, so Calum suggested a system by which we assessed any new referral within two weeks of the GP writing to us. At that session we would assess for risk of self-harm or harm to others and in consultation with the client's GP take any immediate action needed. We would also offer appropriate self-help material so the client had something to be working with until they eventually got to see us; at that point perhaps six weeks to two months later. Average waiting lists in health centres in some parts of England and Wales were six months to a year.

Counsellors who work to the ethics and good practice guidelines of the British Association of Counselling and Psychotherapy (BACP) must have regular supervision, at least one hour and a half hours a month. We all had individual supervision. There was a lack of qualified and experienced supervisors in Shetland so Tracy and I chose to have supervisors from the UK mainland who we spoke to monthly by telephone. We also had regular peer supervision where we could share any issues that were causing us concern.

Confidentiality was of course paramount and clients' names were never disclosed. Clients' issues sometimes trigger one's own 'stuff' and this space was an opportunity to talk through how that might impact on the work with a client. Calum always made himself available to share his experience and expertise and he was very generous in this respect, despite the demands on his time as service manager. We were encouraged to refer clients on to the community mental health team or to specialist services on the UK mainland if we felt the referral was outside our own protocol or individual expertise.

It was the administrative side of the job that was becoming tedious and frustrating. We used an evaluation tool called CORE that was evidence based and could be used to analyse and demonstrate how a client improved or otherwise by the end of counselling. It was a useful tool to support the value of our work and reflect on practice, but IT and interface with NHS systems continued to be an issue. Lack of financial resources meant we were expected to be more or less individually self-sufficient in all admin. This was time consuming and limited offering our expertise of group work, training or consultancy elsewhere to the Shetland

Health Board, Islands Council or Voluntary Sector. In the team it was leading to some dissatisfaction.

'Do you fancy coming clubbing tonight?' Rhys asked me one evening in December.
'Clubbing? You don't like dancing and loud noise, remember?'
'Film Club is on tonight.'
'Oh, right.'
'Let me check my diary... Fine, I hope the sound's better this time.'
We got in the car and drove towards Scalloway via Tingwall Loch.
'Oh look, there's a family playing music in their front room.' I said, pointing to a small pebble-dash bungalow by the Loch. 'There are a couple of fiddle players, an accordionist and a piano player,'
'Then it's probably the Fiddle and Accordion Club. I've heard they have their weekly jam sessions in the Golf Club.'
Rhys tried to look right as he gripped the steering wheel tightly trying to see the road beyond icy sleet.
'The bad weather doesn't stop Shetlanders going out, does it?' he said.
'No, but I was just thinking about the delights of another cosy night in.'

In Shetland there is a club for anything and everything you can imagine: there are the usual golf, pigeon racers, stroke club etc.; then those which reflect its watery interests, boating, fishing, windsurfing clubs; the Shetland specifics, such as the Northmavine Cattle Compensation Society, Up Helly Aa (I want to be a Viking club) and the Althing Debating Club, based on the original Viking parliament and discussing issues such as, 'Shetlanders are obsessed with Vikings.'

If you wanted to go dancing you joined the Shetland traditional dance club. If you wanted to throw yourself around the floor in an unstructured sort of way you would go to the British Legion. If you were young you might avoid the British Legion and look for the sign with men at work wearing pulsating ear muffs. If you were older and worried about going deaf then you would avoid club signs with pulsating ear muffs. On the other hand, if you had inadvertently overlooked the pulsating ear muffs you could find yourself in the Deaf Club.

A week later Rhys and I were invited to the Philosophy Club by Roger. This was a very select club to which you had to be individually invited by a member. Our office base was on the first floor near to the kitchen ward where Roger, a musician masquerading as a domestic worked. I first heard Roger before I met him as Roger whistled while he worked. I was feeling a bit homesick one day and followed the source of the music like a child following the Pied Piper. I found a small wiry seventy year old with a thatch of grey hair curling to a peak above his tiny frame, up to his elbows in soapy water, his lips pursed like a blackbird, whistling his heart out to a Beatles' song on Radio 4's Desert Island Discs.

Roger had had an interesting life teaching young people with behavioural problems in liberal education establishments in England and Scotland. He was also an accomplished classical musician and avid reader. At lunchtime in the canteen he could be seen nearing the end of a large serious tome, while munching his way through a mountain of vegetables. This should have been a warning. Since retirement as a teacher he had been working as a domestic. He enjoyed the work and it also gave him a small income. Roger had started the Philosophy Club with Jack, a Shetlander, about thirty years ago, two brilliant young men who did not wish to end up like everyone else talking about the weather.

'You should be very flattered,' Gerrie said, when I told her. 'I've never been asked and I think of Jack as a surrogate father.'

We *were* very flattered especially because the weather was the main topic of our daily conversation. We knew nothing about philosophy and were therefore somewhat nervous but very pleased to be widening our social circle.

On the night we were the first to arrive and invited to sit in a semi-circle in Roger's front room. There were musical instruments and books everywhere. Soon other members started to arrive. Jack led the discussion and had made copious notes on the meeting's theme of 'mind and body'. He had worked for the Meteorological Office, so no wonder he'd had enough of talking about the weather. Apart from Roger and Jack, other members at the meeting included a retired teacher and her lover, and a Dutch surgeon and his pregnant Iranian wife, who worked in prosthetics. It was very difficult to hide in the small meeting even if we were seated behind a grand piano covered in old hospital blankets. Fortunately, the surgeon's English was superb and he was well informed, working on mind and body most days. By the end of the evening the question of how the brain differed from the mind remained an unresolved question and one I hoped I would not have to address at the next meeting.

'Hi Mum. How are you?'

'We're fine, Liam,' I said trailing the phone into the lounge and curling up on the settee. 'What about you?'

'I've got mumps.'

Can't they make a young man sterile?

'Oh no! How did you get them?'

'They're going the rounds. There's also been a meningitis scare.'

The French kissing disease.

'Are you alright? Have you seen a doctor? You had better come home.'

'If I go home I could give it to Rachel or the lodger.'

'What about coming up here?'

'What for?'

Oh yes, home for you is still Taffs Well, not where we are.

'So we can look after you.'

'I've been told to go home by Uni, my glands are still up so I've put myself into quarantine.'

'What do you mean?'

'I want to go to Switzerland snowboarding in a few days, so I've told friends not to come near me. I'm staying in my room.'

'What are you doing for food?'

'Some of the guys are leaving stuff by the door.'

Sounds hygienic.

'How's your course?'

'I haven't been for a week, but about the same, boring.'

'Any progress with other subjects?'

'I don't want to talk about it at the moment. Look, I've gotta go.'

'Alright Liam. I'll call you soon. Love you.'

'Love you too, Mum, love to Dad. Byeee.'

I was ready for a break. Lerwick was getting ready for the festive season with lights in the street and the shops filling with spangle and sparkle. We had promised Rachel that we would come home for Christmas but we wanted to return for Hogmanay, having never experienced a Scottish new year's eve and Maggie and Bob had invited us around for 'first footing'.

'When are you leaving?' Calum asked me.

'On the 23rd.'

'Not a good idea. You need to give yourself at least another day, just in case of bad weather.'

'But I don't have enough leave.'

'Don't worry about that. I'm sure you will make up the time when you return, won't you? You wouldn't want to miss out on Christmas with the family, would you?'

Another gold star for you, boss. Come here and give us a kiss.

'Let's have people over to reciprocate before we go home,' I suggested to Rhys one morning as I was getting ready for work.

'Good idea. What were you thinking of?'

'A lunch party for the counselling team before Tracy goes down south for her op and perhaps an evening drink for the neighbours. I've got to rush but let's talk about it tonight.'

I have a tendency to get very anxious before entertaining. If I am under a lot of stress I can get vicious with Rhys. Whatever he does isn't good enough, small running sores of resentment can build to a crescendo of nastiness and so it was a couple of days before the lunch party.

'For God's sake Rhys, can't you prioritise? I know you want to finish the painting you're working on, but if I don't get started on the cooking I'll be exhausted before the day. Where are the things I asked you to buy?'

'I'm sorry, I...' he blushed.

'You know I'm tired and low. This isn't helping.'

'I'm sorry, I...'

Speak up, man.

'I promise, I'll go and do it tomorrow.'

'It's not fucking good enough.'

He blushed with humiliation.

Isn't this a teeny weeny bit over the top? Stop now.

'Janet, come on now. Calm down,' he coaxed.

I don't want to.

'Can't you do anything right?' I shouted and flounced out of the kitchen.

Was that my mother talking?

'I'm sorry Rhys. I was a shit last night. How do you put up with me?' I said remorsefully the following morning as I stirred porridge on the stove.

It's like I'm testing you.

'It's alright, but please don't swear at me.'

When does the abused stop protecting the abuser?

'Quick, put this in your freezer,' rasped Emily as she and Donald dashed from their car like burglars getting rid of stolen goods. I grabbed the tea cloth wrapped parcels.

'They're icy. Is this from your little man?' I whispered.

'It's a house warming present. You'd think a dead lamb would be bigger than this, wouldn't you?

'Here's a home-made lemon cheese cake, an almond apple sponge and some cream,' said Gerrie, coming into the kitchen. That smells nice, what is it?'
It's a mess. Please ex chef, thank you for your great gifts, but get out of the kitchen and give me a break.

'Well, everyone seemed to enjoy themselves,' said Rhys a few hours later as he scraped the detritus of the party off our landlady's plates. 'We've still got loads of food left, perhaps we should have Maggie and Bob over for supper?

'Yes, but there's not much time before we leave. We'll do that in the new year. Pity Donald was pinned in at the table by Calum for most of the afternoon. He's an interesting guy, I would have liked to have talked to him more.'

'Yes, I think so would have a few others. I do like your colleagues though.'

'Here's a little minding, a hansel,' Violet said, as she stepped into the hall dead on 8pm a few nights later.

'Little minding? Hansel?'
Where's Gretel?

'They're Shetland words for gifts - a housewarming present.'

Bobby and Margaret followed her into the living room.

'No Michael?'

'No, he's a lovely man, he'd do anything for you, but he's not very comfortable in social situations like this.'

'Oh, someone's been baking,' said Margaret, thrusting another hansel in to my hand.

Yes, a huge risk. You'll probably now understand why I'm reluctant to join the SRWI.

Bobby sat himself slowly into one of the armchairs and told us about their crofting days.

'You could nae live by the croft alone. We had a few acres, kept animals and grew vegetables. I've been a merchant seaman and also drove long distance lorries for years. Violet nursed. You had to, to survive.'

'We had this opportunity to live here. It's perfect for us, easy to keep clean and warm. The croft could be draughty,' Violet said. 'We've been here for the past six or seven years. We're really happy here.'

Violet and Bobby looked at each other and smiled in a way that suggested that even after fifty years of being married they were still very much in love with each other.

I looked at Rhys leaning over to hear what Margaret was saying about her late husband.

Will we have what it takes to be like Violet and Bobby?

The 22nd of December arrived.

'I've had a hell of a day," I said, as I came through the door. 'That Dr Rose sent me an e-mail accusing me of playing ping pong with her patients. She was so angry. I wondered if she'd picked up some of the resentment I feel against her and the rest of the doctors, who've shown such little interest in me.'

Rhys was standing in his studio with his coat on putting the finishing touches to a painting of a Viking Settlement.

'What did you do?'

'I was fuming but I waited until my own anger subsided and then I e mailed her back and asked if I could come and speak to her. I summoned up all my mediation skills, but she apologised before I started and anyway, to cut a long story short, I told her exactly how I was feeling.'

'Good job we're getting off the island tonight then!' Rhys put his paint brush down and wrapped his arms around me.

'Changing the subject, how long do you think it took the Vikings to get home from Shetland?

'Probably not as long as it will take us,' I said, thinking of the fourteen hours on the Northlink Ferry to Aberdeen, the three hours by Megabus to Edinburgh, the bus to the airport, BMI Baby cheapo flight to Cardiff, bus from airport to Cardiff city centre and finally, bus to Taff's Well and home, a mere 20 odd hours if everything went on time.

Rhys put our cases in the car, which we would leave at the Ferry terminal in Lerwick. In our excitement we laughed and joked about what a great Christmas this would be. We were all smiles and grins as we waved goodbye to our kit house.

Wales, here we come!

It was very dark as we drove out of Strand Loch and on to the main north road and the five mile stretch into Lerwick. I stared at my reflection in the car window. My face had filled out with all the good food I'd been putting away. I looked tired but my chest was fluttering in anticipation of going home. I peered out into the darkness. One or two Shetland ponies huddled together by the side of the road, their long hair waving across their nodding faces like singers in a heavy metal band.

Goodbye ponies, see you in a week

As we sped towards the town in the eerie light the swishing blades of the windmills resembled arms of aerobic giants.

Goodbye windmills.

As we came over the brow of the hill and looked down, the few lights of the island of Bressay twinkled in the distance across the sound. In the foreground to the left we could see the bold illuminated lettering of Shetland Catch's large fish processing operation, and in front of us the lights of a variety of boats in the harbour.

'What time did you say the ferry for Aberdeen leaves?' Rhys asked.

'7pm.'

'Then why isn't it in the harbour?'

'Perhaps it hasn't arrived yet."

'But it arrives in the early morning and sits in the harbour all day ready for its return to Aberdeen in the evening.'

'OK. Don't panic Mr Mannering! Let's go and park and see if we can find it. It's a huge vessel, perhaps it's docked further down or perhaps it's late because of the weather.'

As we ran across to the ferry terminal building there was no large sparkly ferry to be seen. The building was also in complete darkness.

'The bastards, they've cancelled the ferry and not told us,' I said, ready to throw the blame anywhere I could.

'Look at the ticket,' Rhys said, his face starting to twitch with anxiety.

I know what you're thinking. I'm thinking the same. We're not going to get home for Christmas.

'Oh shit!, I said, reading the small print on the ticket under the gloom of the parking lot light. 'The ferry left at 5.30pm. It does that twice a week as it stops off at Orkney. That's what makes it a fourteen rather than a twelve hour journey.'

We got in the car and headed back to Strand Loch.

Hello windmills
Hello ponies
Hello darkness, my old friend.

I noticed an anonymous neighbour's curtain twitch as we pulled up at the house.

Yes, have a good look. We're back and we might be inviting ourselves over for Christmas.

The nice young Orcadian woman I spoke to on the phone said it was 'nae problem' to change as we weren't needing a cabin. Although, she did ask me if I was sure about that. It can be difficult without a cabin if it's a rough crossing,' she added.

'We don't mind, we're used to roughing it. We just want to get home for Christmas,' I said, like a character out of 'It's a wonderful life.'

The following evening we set out again for the Northlink ferry terminal.

'If you'd made a mistake like that Rhys, I'd have given you hell. So why didn't you? I deserved it,' I said, as we later settled down to attempt to sleep on the long seats in the ferry lounge bar.

'They'd be little point. You didn't do it on purpose and it's all sorted now. Chris is meeting us in Edinburgh and driving us to the airport. The weather is fine, so fingers crossed, it will be close but we should be home for Christmas.'

You are one cool dude and I don't deserve you.

As we put on our black-out masks and snuggled down into our sleeping bags the Shetlanders and the soothmoothers in the bar were already whooping it up for Christmas.

I wonder if Rachel has bought a turkey?

'I bought a turkey,' said Rachel, as she threw our wheelie cases into the boot of the old Fiesta we had lent her while we were away in Shetland. We had had an on-schedule ferry ride to Aberdeen, the connecting buses to Edinburgh and the plane were on time. Chris did his bit. So, there we were at 4pm on Christmas Eve in Cardiff International Airport. We'd arrived and it had taken a mere 21hours since starting off the previous day from Strand Loch.

'But I haven't managed to get much else,' she added.

'First stop Tesco then,' Rhys said, as he looked at me and winked.

It might be bit of a frugal Christmas then.

Seeing our house after a few months seemed strange. The grass in the front garden looked lush and straggly. The Garth Mountain loomed over us in the twilight.

'I'll have to do the lawn and the hedge before we go back,' said Rhys as we opened the front gate. Then, as we opened the front door,

'Hey, Rachel the house is looking clean. Is this all your own work?'

'Yes.'

'Where's the lodger?'

'She's in Spain with her parents.'

'How have things been?'

'Don't ask.'

We had our Christmas with most of the trimmings, well those we could still buy before the shops shut.

'I'm so glad you've come home for Christmas,' said Rachel as we toasted each other opening our presents. Pity Liam isn't with us.'

I saw Rhys blink.

'What do they say about Mohammed and the mountain?' I said.

'I will come up to see you guys, probably in the spring.'

'No problem. Let's enjoy the time we have together now.'

'Do you know how many are coming to your party? She asked.

We had decided to throw a party on the 28th of December for our friends and family and sent out email invitations some time before. I didn't want to repeat my pre-entertainment performance of a couple of weeks before so we decided to keep it relatively simple. It also meant we could spend the next couple of days with Rachel walking on the Garth and in the snowy Brecon Beacons.

'You look well,' my sister-in-law said.
I've put on weight?
'You've got that glow of the outdoors.'
You mean, fat.
'So what's it like?' our guests asked as they tucked into the cold buffet.

'Very different from here.'

They were all eager to know more about our Shetland adventure and poured over our photos and asked lots of questions.

'It looks bleak.'

'It can be, but some of the views are stunning and the light'

'Oh, you do see the light?' a friend asked.

Everyone laughed.

'From around 10am to 3pm at the moment, but in the summer it will be all day and most of the night.'

'Have you met lots of incomers running away from something?' asked another friend.

Is that what you think we're doing?

'I guess there are people like that, but the people we've met seem to be there for a good reason.'

Like us. I'm not running away from something, am I? I'm running towards the experience, trying to embrace it, aren't I?

'What are the Shetlanders like?'

'They're friendly and welcoming. Some of the men are more reserved, shy of incomers perhaps.'

'You are brave. Not sure we could do that.'

A little group looked at each other and nodded.

'Will you ever come back?'

Didn't I make it clear when we left? We're going for a year and then we'll see.

'What did you think?' Rhys asked, as he poured us another glass of wine and started the party post mortem.

'Everyone seemed genuinely pleased to see us. I felt more appreciated than I think I ever have before.'

'The fact that so many came and some from a long distance too.'

'Yes, it's meant a lot. I'm going to miss our family and friends. Not that we see much of them normally.'

'No, you don't fully appreciate something until you no longer have it, do you?'

A doubt about long-term prospects like a worm without direction began its squirming and we'd been away for less than three months.

The night before we were due to leave Rachel and I were having a girly chat on her bed.

'I wish you and Liam could be up there with us.'

'Well, that's not going to happen.'

'No, I guess not. What's the term looking like for you?'

'Hectic. I've got an assignment to hand in before teaching starts and my timetable's looking busier than ever. They're piling on the work. I'll be glad when this year's over.'

And it hasn't even yet begun.

'Look darling, don't worry about coming to the airport tomorrow. It's a very early start. We'll get a taxi and I'll say goodbye now.'

I gave her a special rib-breaking hug reserved for abandoned daughters.

'Love you. Hopefully, see you soon. Take care of yourself.'

'You too, Mum. Safe journey.'

I left the filial warmth of Rachel's room, walked down a few stairs and opened my son's bedroom door. Nothing much had changed since September, when he left for Uni. He'd only come back once that term and his bed had that rumbled look of a duvet pulled over in haste.

Wonder how many Swiss youths were a snowboard away from catching the mumps?

The taxi arrived at five thirty am on the 30th to take us to the airport. We caught the 7am flight to Edinburgh airport, bus to Edinburgh, a few hours wait and bus to Aberdeen, walked from the bus station to the ferry terminal, slept in the lounge bar of the Northlink ferry to Lerwick, then picked up our car and drove to Strand Loch. Arrival time: 7am, New Year's Eve. Total travel time: twenty five and a half hours; the time it would take to fly to Australia. Cost for two people, approximately £200. If we had flown it would have been more like £750 and would have taken less than a few hours.

After a quick early morning shower I went straight back to work in Lerwick until around 4pm when things in the health centre began to get quiet. Then, after a few hours sleep we got ourselves ready to go 'first footing' and Rhys drove the 15 miles up to Maggie and Bob's croft near Voe.

Their croft is 'betwixt the hills'in remote countryside with wonderful views of the sea. Maggie's great-grand and grandparents had been crofters and had been moved during the clearances of the nineteenth and early twentieth centuries. This croft had been handed down to her (although theoretically still owned by the Crofter's Commission). Maggie and Bob had built a new house alongside the original croft house, had sheep, chickens, dogs and cats, plus land on which they had valiantly planted hundreds of deciduous trees. They were still pretty small due to the elements but over the past years since returning to live in Shetland they had been determined to develop a habitat for local and migratory birds.

'First footing' involves visiting your neighbours and friends late on New Year's Eve/early New Year's morning. You take a selection of drinks with you to offer and in return they dispense their hospitality, drink, food and company.

'Does she like reestit mutton?' May, an elderly neighbour asked Maggie in the first croft we visited.

'I've never tried it,' I said, remembering Bob's detailed description of how he had pickled, salted and left to mature the objects looking like fake hams hanging on the clothes line in their kitchen. An open sandwich of fatty mutton was placed in my hand.

'It's not to everyone's taste,' May said, smiling broadly.

'Looks delicious,' I lied.

God, how am I going to eat this. Try and be polite. Smile!

May and Alex had been crofting for the past seventy odd years. Their small living room was warm and cosy. Alex was shy and reserved like many Shetland men we had met. He sat in the corner by the peat fire, a broad face without lines, looking well scrubbed and wearing a hand knitted Shetland woollen jumper.

'How old do you think Alex is?' Bob asked me.

Alex looked away.

I haven't a clue.

'Go on, how old do you think?' Maggie urged.

'Seventy?'

'He's eighty-nine.'

'Never!'

'That's the crofting life for you, Janet,' laughed Maggie.

'I'm eighty two,' added May sociably.

May was widely travelled and had a silver tea spoon collection displayed on her wall to prove it. There was even a wooden map of Australia decorated with spoons.

'Those cups in the cupboard are her trophies won for indoor bowls,' Maggie said.

I slowly bit small pieces of mutton trying to swallow and not taste the greasy meat. I gulped at my red wine to disguise the taste. Rhys, on the other hand seemed to be enjoying his sandwich and was eating with gusto.

He's good at being polite and not hurting other people's feelings. Why does my face say exactly what's going on inside?

'Is it alright?' May asked in a concerned voice.

'Very good, thank you,' he said, as he turned his good ear to Alex. 'This ear doesn't work very well.' Rhys put his right finger in his left ear.

'I have the same problem,' Alex replied, cupping his hand behind his fleshy ear.

This 'first footing' reminded me of the time twenty five years before, when Rhys first took me home to meet his relatives in rural Wales. I must have eaten six cream teas in one afternoon as every home got out the best china and did their best to welcome me. I remembered that nauseous feeling wondering if I could hold on to the contents of my stomach until we got outside.

Come on, buck up. You'll offend these nice people. You can finish this sandwich.

'Come on, time to go, I'm afraid,' said Bob, pummelling Alex' hand with his naval grip.

'Happy New Year!' Bob picked up his bag of booze and we bid them farewell.

'Do call again,' said May cheerfully at the door.

We got in the car and Bob drove us into Voe village and to the home of their friends Kathleen and Peter.

'Peter is the local grave-digger and endearingly referred to locally as one part of the infamous 19th century body snatching duo,' said Maggie, as we waited for someone to answer the front door of the smart new house. We were introduced and Kathleen dashed into the kitchen and busied herself with making sandwiches.

'What will you have to drink?' Bob asked all of us.

'No, let me get something for your friends first,' Kathleen called. 'What will you have?'

'Peter is very well travelled,' Maggie said as we sipped our drinks. Peter smiled coyly.

'Where have you travelled, Peter?' I asked, taking my cue.

'Faroes, Greenland, Iceland. I'm hoping to go to Canada next year.' He looked at his watch.

'Yes, it still is this year, just!' Kathleen said, putting plates of home bakes on the table.

'All places north.' Rhys said.

'Yes, you'll find because of our Scandinavian connection, many Shetlanders are more interested in exploring the northern hemisphere than the south,' said Maggie.

'Mind you,' added Bob, 'many Shetlanders you meet are well travelled because of fishing and the sea.

You might expect parochialism on small islands but I have never found that here.'

'No, it's true. We're very interested in the outside world,' said Peter.

'What about you, Kathleen? Do you enjoy travelling?' I asked.

'Heck no, I leave all that to Peter,' she laughed.
The opposite of May and Alex; May was the traveller and Alex stayed home.

'Now, have you tried this local delicacy? Kathleen said, pointing to the sandwiches. 'Don't be shy. Tuck in.'

After a short while Bob looked at his watch, giving us the signal to get ready to take our leave.

'Happy New Year!' we all shouted to Kathleen and Peter, as we ran out into the cold night air once again.

'Are you enjoying yourselves?' Maggie asked.

'Yes, great!' said Rhys.

'Where to next, Maggie?' I asked. 'This is fun.'

'To my cousin-in-law's, Chrissy. It's not far.'

'If you dig a little you'll find that Maggie is related to most folk around here,' Bob teased.

'Yes, I've been doing my family tree. It's fascinating.' Maggie pulled out a shiny lipstick from a small evening bag and freshened her make-up.

We arrived at a row of semis and tumbled out of the car while Bob found somewhere to park. We entered a smoky living room with the TV was on full blast. A few women were watching the screen.

'Happy New Year!' Maggie said to everyone. Chrissy came forward and brushed Maggie's cheek. A row of roly-poly fishermen, red-faced and sausage fingered nodded to us and invited us to sit down.

'Will you have a dram, Bob?' one said.

'No thanks, I'm driving, but I'm sure Rhys and Janet will.' We nodded enthusiastically and someone brought a couple of glasses. The fisherman was very generous with his servings of amber malt. Bob chatted with him for a while and then again gave us the signal and off we went.

We arrived at the steps of a bungalow as a crowd of people tumbled down towards us laughing and wishing us the best of the season. It was now New Year's Day. We were welcomed by an elderly couple and introduced to families sitting politely round the edge of their 1960's decorated living room as if it was a dentist's surgery. The husband poured us a drink and his wife thrust an open mutton sandwich into our hands. I smiled and watched Rhys eat voraciously.

Not sure I can do this.

I was distracted by a young man in leathers, who engaged us in conversation about his forthcoming trip around South America on a motorbike.

'Just like Che Guevara,' I said.

'Yes, it was the film about his life, 'Motor Cycle Diaries,' that inspired my plans.'

I see what Bob means about Shetlanders and travel.

We eventually wobbled back to Maggie and Bob's in the early hours of the morning and slept well. It had been a great night.

Shetland Ponies

January 2005

'Violet's invited us to a senior citizens Christmas do in Tingwall Public Hall,' Rhys said a couple of nights later. Look, here's the invite. It's to celebrate Auld Christmas.'

'Auld Christmas?'

'In the Julian calendar Christmas is on the 8th of January.'

'Am I showing my age that much?'

'It's me, who's the senior citizen. You're invited as my escort.'

'Well, that's alright then.'

We arrived to find that there had been a mix up about starting times and all the old folk had already finished their roast dinner and were on to their jelly and ice cream. The organisers fussed about and produced two places and two dinners, which we realised afterwards must have been intended for the women serving. As we tucked in we got chatting to others on our table, hands cupped behind ears and heads bent low in efforts to hear each other. One elderly man told us about his time stationed in Wales during the war and tried out words of a remembered language.

'Rwyn dy garu di,' he said in a broad Shetland accent.

I love you, eh? Bet that got you into lots of Welsh knickers, you old rascal.

After the meal was cleared away we sat around the edge of the hall waiting for the entertainment. It started with a storyteller who droned on in dialect some story involving a donkey getting in and out of a cottage. Everyone who understood it laughed a lot. Then there was a band led by a woman who had won the young fiddler of the year award. We all tapped our feet as the woman of my own age, who hadn't had any dinner, served us drams of whisky and boiled sweets; an interesting combination and one that I'd not tried before.

A few nights later there was a gale Force 12; a so-called hurricane on the Beaufort wind scale that I had pinned by the front door. The gales were becoming relentless. We closed the curtains and cosied down for lots of nights in. There was something exciting and dramatic about hearing the rain and the wind beat like frenzied African drumming against the windows of our kit house. Then we thought of the fishermen out in the North Sea and the Atlantic; not quite so romantic.

I was very busy with clients during the days and didn't have much time to think about home but the evenings dragged. There was too much time to loll on the sofa, twirling my hair around my finger pretending to read, but reflecting on that worm of doubt and where it might be leading. In some ways, although going home, seeing and touching those who I missed so much had been reassuring and validating, it had also made that black hole of longing a little deeper. I decided to continue my art therapy sessions with Freya.

We agreed on early morning sessions before I started work. I would arrive at her studio around 7.45am and invariably she would arrive around the same time, puffing from running, her hair wet from showering, apologizing profusely. I found the routine comforting. She would put on the kettle, switch on the fire and sit down in a big armchair. I sat on the sofa in my coat, hat and gloves until I warmed up. Then, she would ask me if I'd like to sit at the table and while I poured my heart out, she poured out primary colours into a pallet and invited me to take up a brush.

On that first session of the new year we discussed the incident before Christmas with Dr Rose.
'How did it make you feel?' Freya asked, sitting beside me watching me paint.
'I was so angry with her.'
'And?'
'I've done my best to work professionally with her patients and keep her informed. The idea that I would play ping-pong with them'
'Yes?'
'I felt unjustly criticized.'
'How did your parents do feelings when you were a child?'

'My father was affectionate. There was warmth and laughter but tension and anger is the main feeling I remember in the home.'

'How did your parents manage conflict?'

'I suppose I was provocative as a teenager. I would taunt my mother. I remember cowering in the corner of the kitchen, my mother raining slaps down on me.'

'What about your brother?'

'He was seven years younger than me. He could do no wrong with her.'

Freya nodded, her green eyes encouraging me to go on.

'Looking back, I was probably jealous of him. I'd been the centre of my parents' world until he came along.'

'And the way you got their attention?'

'I suppose mainly by picking an argument. I don't think I'm doing that with the doctors in the health centre though.'

'Can you see any connection?'

'Yes, I can now. It's the same rage of feeling invisible and at the same time somehow needing their approval.'

'Paint your feelings.'

I ran the brush over the page in spirals of colour.

'How does that feel?

'I feel a sense of relief actually, just understanding that there could be a connection. Thank you Freya.'

When I got into the health centre and turned on my computer there was an e-mail waiting for me from the Welsh speaking GP. He asked me if I could let him know when I was free, he wanted to speak to me. I replied immediately and within a few minutes there was a knock on the counselling door. He looked a bit awkward.

'Did you have a nice Christmas?' he asked.
Dr Rose has had a word with him.
'Yes, thank you. Did you?'
'We stayed here. My parents came up.'
That's interesting. Perhaps he's come up here to get away from them.
'I understand that you've been feeling.. err..'
Perhaps he doesn't do feelings either.
'Not that happy, not part of the 'team.'
'Yes, that's right. I feel part of the counselling team but not part of the health centre team.'
'You need to understand that until very recently there hasn't really been a 'team.' GPs rented space in this building. We're now employees of the Shetland Health Board and we're trying to weld together a team of disparate services.'
Now it starts to make sense.
'Oh, I see.'

'How can we make it better for you?'

Invite me home for dinner, show some interest in me as a person and speak to my husband in Welsh.

'Perhaps we could come to team meetings and give you regular updates on your patients we're counselling?'

'Yes, sure. E-mail is great but it doesn't have the personal touch, does it?

'No, absolutely.'

He put his hand on the door handle, ready to leave, when he suddenly remembered something.

'My patients have said some good things about your work, by the way.'

At last, some positive feedback.

'That's good to know, thank you.'

He went out and closed the door behind him, but then immediately popped his blonde head back round the door as he remembered something else.

'How's Tracy? When is she coming back? I have some new referrals.'

Diolch yn fawr. Thank you very much, doctor.

Shetland ceased to be part of the Danish empire and became part of Scotland in 1469. The daughter of King Christian of Denmark, who also ruled Norway and Sweden married the son of James 11. The Scots demanded a dowry which included Orkney and Shetland. Despite recent Scottish devolution and Edinburgh being the seat of government, Shetlanders see themselves as Shetlanders first and foremost; in many cases the Norse connection demonstrated through their history, language and dialect suggests a closer relationship to Scandinavia than Scotland.

Mid January is the start of the Shetland fire festivals having roots in Scandinavian and Celtic fire festivals and a Shetland tradition of 'guizing' or dressing up. The current 'Up-Helly-Aa' as it is known locally is a nineteenth century invention, where men of Shetland dress as Vikings and guizers, parade through the streets with flaming tar torches, singing as they follow the boat they have spent most of the winter making, only to see it burn at the end of the procession. It is also a good excuse to grow a beard, drink and make merry in the depressing mid-winter. The festivals start in Scalloway in January and take place in most of the communities and islands over the weeks until March.

'May I come to Up-Helly-Aa in Scalloway with you?' asked Maggie, when she and Bob came over for supper one evening. 'I haven't been to that one for some years.'

'I'm off to France house-sitting for a few weeks, looking after a naval officer's place, while he goes on holiday. I'm told that it is good bird watching country,' Bob said.

'You don't want to go Maggie?' I asked.

'I'd love to but someone's got to look after the croft and the animals. Anyway, it is good for Bob to have a break. He won't be alone much. Rebecca, our daughter is going out for a week's visit.'

Ah, that's a good idea. Breaks up winter and probably helps the relationship.

'By all means Maggie. It will be good to have you join us.'

The following Friday evening, January 14th, Maggie called and we set off for Scalloway. It was a bitterly cold evening.

'Here's the galley shed,' Maggie said, as we strolled down the main street. 'It's where the men get away from their wives and girlfriends all winter in the pretence of building the boat.'

Suddenly, we saw the procession heading our way.

'Look, doesn't the castle look dramatic lit up? said Rhys.

'Yes,' replied Maggie, 'but the castle ruin is a grim reminder of the cruel reign of the Stewart earls back in the sixteenth and seventeenth centuries. Come on let's squeeze in.'

We got in line, following the Vikings' flaming torches, wiry and wild in the wind. Their helmets and shields shone in the tar light, the men looking intent on rape and pillage just as soon as they'd burnt their boat. They marched to the Up-Helly-Aa song about victorious Viking heroes, led by a band of Scottish kilted drummers, who presumably they had caught on a previous raid and put to good use.

'Rhys, you're on fire!' I shouted, as I beat down the sparks on his anorak with my gloved hands. I noticed that there was a lot of other beating going on around us.

'Oh my God, that woman in front, her hair is alight!'

Fortunately, someone else also saw this in time and doused her with a water bottle they were carrying presumably for the purpose, because it was whisky not water you'd want to drink on a night like that.

The Viking boat, about thirty foot long, was a true work of art, beautifully made and painted in bright coloured patterns complete with a mast and large dragon's head. When we got to the end of the village by the boat club, the Vikings lined up dramatically and after a 1-2-3 tossed their flaming torches into the boat. The eyes of the dragon looked surprised momentarily, then its jaw dropped, bearing its white pointy teeth and fell into a great bonfire throwing light and sparks on to other small boats bobbing innocently close by in the bay.

'Don't grieve for the boat,' said Maggie, seeing the look on our faces 'Come on, the next bit should be a lot of fun.'

We made our way to Tingwall Village Hall, where the other part of the evening was about to begin. Local men and women had formed themselves into squads and were about to perform their acts. As we entered the packed hall we heard the whirr of the fiddle and accordion. We looked around for seats. No luck, then a tall bearded bloke got up and beckoned. I looked behind me to see who he was beckoning.

'Oh, it's Jim and his family', said Rhys pointing the way across the empty dance floor. Jim was a local architect, who we met when we walked over his land not knowing if there was a public footpath through it or not. In England and Wales folk can be funny about trespass and it was with a little trepidation that we first met.

'In Shetland you can walk more or less where you want,' he'd said, in broad dialect, 'as long as you don't have dogs. They worry the sheep'

'We don't have a dog.'

'Then feel free,' he'd said, in a gesture that suggested that all this land would be ours one day if we were related to him, which unfortunately we weren't. He had rebuilt a croft house, despite it being more expensive to do so, rather than building a new house like most would have done. He had renovated it using modern environmentally friendly techniques. His view over the Loch and towards the sea was spectacular. To the right below, you could see three large rings, indicating farmed salmon fishing and often seals could be seen scouting around the feeder boat. Beyond, was the coastline of Nesting on the east of the mainland and tiny rocks peeping up like sea water frogs checking out the action. Jim was a shy modest man in his 40's, who was making an effort with incomers. We appreciated him immediately.

We squashed in by the rest of his family, his partner, a physiotherapist and their two sons, aged 10 and 12. Meanwhile, Jim managed to get to the bar and pretty quickly he had put large drinks in to our hands.

'How did you get on selling your landscapes at the farmer's market?' he asked, as we waited for the entertainment. Jim was on the hall committee and had helped Rhys put up a table.

'Lots of people showed interest, but no-one bought.'

'Give it time. People may need to get to know you first.'

The Scalloway Up-Helly-Aa differs from the Lerwick one in the sense that women are allowed to take part in the sketches performed by the squads. The hall hushed as the first act came in on their hands and knees hunched under a large black cloth. A female narrator held up a sign entitled 'Which Road Sign?' We all peered and the more astute among the audience, or perhaps those who'd seen it before, shouted out possibilities. At last someone got it in dialect.

'What was that?' I asked Jim's wife, a phrase I was to repeat incessantly that evening.

Poor Rhys, with his hearing he doesn't stand a chance. Who said it would get easier? Shetland dialect is a foreign language.

'Sleeping policemen.'

I guess it's easy to see humps in the road when they are pointed out to you.

The entertainment went on in that vein, with lots of parodies of local characters, councillors and shopkeepers. There were song and dance acts including a bunch of people dressed as white bearded trolls. One squad re-enacted themselves drinking in their local. Everyone thought it was hilarious. We didn't understand a word. In between the acts the band played and most people got up and danced, mainly the Boston two step. Everyone seemed able to dance. Rhys cowered at the prospect of making a fool of himself again.

'I don't know what you're worried about. Most people on the floor tonight have made a fool of themselves in one way or other,' I urged. But he wasn't convinced, so Maggie took me round the dance floor a few times. The rest of the time Rhys and I sat tapping our feet enjoying the rhythms, me wanting to dance, him not.

'It reminds me of the Young Farmers dances in mid Wales,' he said, blushing at the memory. 'I was too shy to ask any girl to dance.'
Why can't you just accept it? He's never going to overcome his anxiety of having pigeon toes. So you might as well give up your ambition to be on Strictly Come Dancing.

Mid way in the evening the Viking Jarl (Earl)'s squad appeared. Each year one squad in turn has the privilege to be the leading elite squad, dressed in expensive deer skin, velvet and carrying pewter-like swords and shields. These outfits cost a small fortune. Men who had grown their beards especially for the event and adolescent boys with stuck on bits of hair, marched seriously around the hall singing the Up-Helly-Aa song. This part wasn't for laughing at.

Who would think that Shetland is no longer part of the great Danish empire?

The acts toured around several other community halls, imbibing large quantities of alcohol en route. Consequently, as the night wore on the acts became less and less comprehensible. The act involving the re-enactment of men drinking in their local were able to drink twice as much as every other act, as they drunk off and on stage. The acts came and went and the band played.

'Going so early?' asked Jim, as we got up to say our goodbyes around midnight.

'What time will it all finish?'

'Probably around 8am tomorrow morning.'

He must think we're right party poopers.

'Have you enjoyed yourselves?'

'Yes, it's been fun, although we've had a bit of difficulty understanding some of the punch lines.'

'Me too!' he laughed.

As we made our way out of the hall, I asked Maggie,

'Is there anywhere you can go to learn Shetland dialect?'

'Yes, I think there's an evening class in Lerwick at the Islesburgh'.

'The class started last September,' a nice woman at the Isleburgh Institute told me on the phone a few days later. 'It's too late for this year, why don't you give me a call later on in the year?'

Since returning from our Christmas in Wales the worm of a doubt began to squirm about our long-term prospects in Shetland. Before going to sleep at night I lay in bed tucked under the 20tog duvet, staring into the cold dark wondering about the future. We'd been away for less than four months, life was interesting, but the short visit had the effect in some ways of making me feel more homesick. As a counsellor I was well aware of the process of transition in my clients' lives. The stages are a bit like a bereavement and even if a transition represents a new opportunity there is usually loss attached in some way. The Chinese pictogram for 'crisis' is a synthesis of 'danger' and 'opportunity,' and that's how it was feeling. Transitions can take any length of time but six to eight months is often needed to work through life events involving significant change and come to a resolution. Bereavements of course can take much much longer.

I noticed that my own therapy was sharpening my understanding and appreciation of the impact of childhood events on those of my clients who were incomers and whose issues included their ability to settle in Shetland. There were some young women clients who had come to Shetland for a romantic reason, the relationship had broken up after a while and they were left not wanting to go home but finding it difficult to stay. There were married clients who had children and who had been well settled with good support networks and friends, but whose marriage had ended and the pull of their own families down south was causing anxiety and procrastination. There were others, who clearly had thought that moving to work far away from a situation such as divorce would be helpful, but because they had suppressed the feelings at the time later found themselves depressed and lonely.

My primary training as a counsellor was as a brief therapist, working in the present, helping clients look to their own resources to find solutions to make their lives better. I sought supervision to assist me work more effectively with clients' early life experiences and in doing so illuminated my own life scripts and coping mechanisms, some of which no longer served me well.

Although working in Lerwick was challenging, working on the outer islands was really growing on me. I loved taking the ferries. The people who worked in the small health centres were friendly and welcoming and I got used to working around the space problems.

One night in mid-January there was a fall of snow. The following morning I drove the fifteen odd miles to the terminal to take the ferry to Whalsay. The air was pure and clean and the sun sparkled on Blue Mull Sound. Thirty or more black shiny coated cormorants played ducking and diving. Large gulls swept down peering in to the awaiting ferry hoping for a snack. The hills around Laxo were like chocolate chip muffins lightly dusted with icing sugar. I breathed in deeply and my spirit soared. I thanked God, the universe and Calum Andrews for giving me all this. How lucky was I!

'And just think,' I said to Rhys on the ferry as we sipped our cappuccinos from the drinks machine, 'if this isn't brilliant enough, they're paying my salary too!'

'Do you want to stay permanently then?'

'I'm still unsure about that. Let's not talk about the future, let's just enjoy the here and now. Anyway, Liam's coming next week, let's see how he likes Shetland.'

On the last Tuesday in January Lerwick celebrates its Up-Helly-Aa, a totally male event. That year it was the 25th of January, the same date as Rachel's birthday. Before going out I phoned her.

'Happy Birthday, darling.'

'Thanks, Mum.'

'Are you going out to celebrate?'

'Doubt it. I have too much work. Maybe at the weekend.'

'Have you had lots of cards and messages from friends and family?'

'I've had some. By the way, have you heard from Liam?'

'Not yet.'

'He's thinking of dropping out of Uni.'

I related the conversation to Rhys in the car on the way to the Up-Helly-Aa celebration in Lerwick.

'Well, we can't do anything about it right now.' His left hand squeezed my hand tightly as he held the steering wheel with his right. 'Cari ti,' he declared.

'Love you too, Rhys.'

That night the normally quiet streets of Lerwick were packed with Vikings and guizers, men dressed as overweight tarts, wearing bubble gum pink blow-up outfits, fat wigged ballerinas in tutus, all kinds of large overweight animals, clowns, school girls, hockey players, in fact every male stereotype fantasy that might involve sex and women. This was certainly a step up in dramatic terms from the fire festival in Scalloway.

We found a place to stand by the park where the Viking galleon would be burnt. Onlookers started to gather, and before long the pavements were packed. It was a still cold starry night, perfect for a procession. Over a thousand Lerwick men were taking part and I don't suppose they all made their own costumes. The total population of Lerwick was around nine and a half thousand, so this event was a huge community affair. A young couple, their arms around each other, were chatting next to us.

'It's called 'Transvestite Tuesday,' you know,' the young man said. They both giggled.

'Have you got the day off tomorrow?'

'Yes, haven't you?'

'I don't work for the SIC, do I?'

'I guess too many people would phone in sick anyway.'

She pulled out a giant bottle of vodka, took a large swig and offered the bottle to her boyfriend.

Eee lass, pass the bottle around, would you?

Suddenly, behind us and up on a scaffolding platform, a band dressed like the Salvation Army started to tune up. Rhys put his finger in his ear. There were wafts of pink smoke emanating from the top of Hill Head by the library. People began to jostle for position to see better. A woman elbowed herself in front of my view.

Geroff woman. I want to see.

Then we saw them; a thousand torches of flaming tar held high above the heads of gleaming helmets and blonde wigs snaking their way down Hill Head , past the Town Hall into King Erik Street and turning left and right into King Harold Street, to and fro they marched in countermotion to the tune of 'Teddy Bears' Picnic.'

'Oh look! the galley,' exclaimed the woman with big elbows, holding a child up to see better.

Women with children first, I know, but I may never see this again.

The Viking galleon was even larger and more spectacular than the one at Scalloway. The boat was striped in black and gold with huge decorated shields on the sides and a tall red and white mast.

'I'm scared of the dragon,' the child whinged.

The blue dragon's head was enormous with a long pointy spine and in the tar light it looked like the Lochness monster. The music changed to the Up-Helly-Aa song, and the Vikings and guizers followed their galley into the park, marching around it in ever increasing circles, until they were all assembled, singing the last verse:

'Our galley is the People's Right, the dragon of the free;

The Right that rising in its might, brings tyrants to their knee;

The flag that flies above us is the Love of Liberty,

The waves are rolling on.'

Then, at a drum roll from the band the marchers got ready and in unison threw their spears of fire onto the galley to produce a magnificent bonfire. The dragon blinked, his head crinkled and slowly fell into the inferno.

'He's gone now,' said the elbows.
Another winter's work gone up in smoke.

'Get a photo, quick Rhys,'
'Where?' whined the child.

'Did you get it?'
'I'm not sure, that child's head'

At about 9pm we made our way to the Town Hall to watch the entertainment. At the front door we were directed upstairs into a large hall with stained glass windows and a highly polished wooden floor. There was a band on a low stage and chairs around the room. You had to leave your booze with your coats and make little trips for fill-ups. We got tired of doing that after a while so kept our drinks hidden in my bag.

The format of the evening was a repeat of Scalloway; itinerant squads presenting their acts, interspersed by music and dancing. Those women eager to dance with a blue elephant or a blow up ballerina sat at the front. We sat at the back. Many of the satirical acts focused on the hot issue of the day, decision making by the Council in regard to failed re-investments of oil revenue. Shetland's oil boom in the 1970s had been used to fund the Islands infrastructure. As a result there was an excellent network of well-maintained roads, leisure centres, health centres and schools. However, some of the investments were doing badly and to balance their books the Council was funding its deficits from reserves. Many Shetland folk felt that the Council was squandering their children's inheritance.

'Up-Helly-Aa was one of the 100 things on our list to do before we pop our clogs,' said a retired

Glaswegian tourist sitting next to us as she pulled her partner up on his feet to do a Boston two step.
Seeing how much you've both drunk so far that might be sooner than you think.

Like many of the Scandinavian countries the long winters certainly drive many to drink to excess. So many of my clients with anxiety and depression also had issues with drink, or members of their families did. Fortunately, there was an excellent alcohol advice and support centre offering specialist help and we worked closely with colleagues there to ensure clients got a good service. Rhys and I found that so many cosy nights in resulted in a bottle of wine when we had only intended to drink a glass. If we weren't careful we could find ourselves at AA meetings, so we made a pact to discourage each other from a second glass. After the Lerwick fire festival it was said that summer would be on its way, the nights get shorter and the sky lightens. We were hoping that would also be a disincentive for another glass.

At midnight there were still over a hundred acts to go and the organisers were predicting the event would go on to around ten the following morning. Then onto the floor came the most bizarre act. Lately, Commercial Street had seen a surfeit of doggy poo. The sketch involved men dressed as large pantomime dogs who were lined up on an identity parade. In order to identify the culprit of the mystery poo, a doctor in a white coat pulled on a pair of white latex gloves and proceeded to give each dog an internal examination.

A few days after 'Up-Helly-Aa' in Lerwick, Liam arrived in Shetland. He had taken his swollen glands off to Switzerland, where he had worked in the kitchen of a hotel throughout the university Christmas break. He hadn't been infectious by the time he arrived there and was soon well enough to spend every spare moment he wasn't washing pots or slicing garlic snowboarding and partying. He had spent the past couple of Christmases out there and we had sort of got used to Christmas without him. However, we hadn't seen him since October when we had taken him out for lunch in Loughborough on our way up to Aberdeen and Shetland. We were very excited.

Lerwick was empty on Sunday morning at 7am when Rhys went down to pick him up off the ferry from Aberdeen. I watched him from the bedroom window as he got out of the car looking tired and unwashed. I ran to the door and bear-hugged him as if I hadn't seen him for four years rather than four months.

'Hey, let me get through the door before you asphyxiate me!' he laughed.

'It's so good to see you Liam,' I blubbed.

'Great to see you too. You look really well.'

You mean fat.

He moved across the kitchen and opened the fridge.

'What's for breakfast?'
Some things don't change

After a hearty Welsh breakfast Liam looked revived and we took him on a tour of some of our favourite places. It was a bitterly cold day and we wrapped up in layers as if we were heading for the North Pole.

'Here's a little present for you,' I said, throwing him a knitted hat.

'Cool,' he said, pulling on the snow crystal patterned hat.'

I better not tell him that I think it's intended for a woman and that it's another charity shop special.

We drove along the edge of Tingwall Loch to Scalloway and showed him where the Shetland Bus had taken off for Norway, then on to Bannamin, our favourite beach on Burra Island. The journey involved first crossing Trondra island, where until the 1970's there had been small ferry boats taking people to and from the mainland and further on to Burra and Bannamin. There was no-one else around. The sea was turbulent, white horses like Pegasus' whole extended family leapt across the water, and waves crashed and smashed against the rocks. There had been a monastery at nearby Papil in the ninth century and the whole place normally had a very tranquil and spiritual feel. That day it was wild.

'This is awesome,' Liam said, as we pushed our palms against each other and leant into the gale force wind, our weather-proofs whistling and flapping against our bodies. 'It's like G force,' he laughed, his freckled cheeks raw and tight straining with the effort.

'Let's go on,' I said. 'and have a closer look at the turquoise sea.'

'Your mother must have been a mermaid in another life,' Rhys shouted at us as we danced along the shoreline, Liam doing Arab springs and back flips, me doing silly walks. The waves pushed and pulled the sandy beach creating a shingly overture we tried to sing along to. It was exhilarating, fun and just wonderful to have Liam there sharing it.

For the next two days while I was working Rhys showed him around. It was an opportunity for them to spend time together, but I felt jealous. I didn't have the leave to take time off. On Monday Rhys took Liam around Lerwick and on Tuesday he came to Yell. Luckily, I had a couple of cancellations so the three of us were able to spend a bit more time together.

Yell is the largest of the North Isles, 17 miles long and up to 7 miles across and is reached by a twenty minute ferry trip across Yell Sound from Toft. The surgery is at Mid Yell and takes a further 15 minutes or so. Travelling by car can offer a good opportunity for talking without appearing too intense. I decided to use the time to find out what was going on for him.

'I had such a good time in Arosa. I didn't want to come back,' he said, as we stood on the deck of the ferry looking back at the mainland.

'You're still not enjoying uni, then?'

'It's the course I'm not enjoying. I didn't have any luck changing. I am thinking of dropping out.'

'And doing what?'

'A season. There's a job in the kitchen in Burestubli if I want it.'

'Would you go back to uni and start another course in October?'

'That's the thing, which course? I'm not sure if I would want to start again with another course I wasn't absolutely sure about. Also, there's the cost.'

'You mean fees and more debt?'

'Yes, I predict if I finish this course and even with your help I'll still owe over £12,000.'

'We're coming into Ulsta. Shall we go down to the car?' Rhys asked.

We got into the car.

'Sit in the front Liam. You'll see better,' I suggested. 'We've got a bit of time, why not take the back road, Rhys?'

'Are you supposed to yell in Yell?' Liam joked.

'Ha ha! I think that may have been said a few times before somehow.'

'Is it all peat bog?' Liam asked after a few minutes.

'It seems like it, but there are some nice beaches, particularly on the West coast.'

We drove on, each in our own internal world.

'There's supposed to be lots of otters on Yell, but we haven't seen one yet,' Rhys said sadly.

'You're wrong, Rhys. Remember the other week? Didn't we catch a glimpse of an otter's backside running into a ditch?'

We all laughed.

'We're coming into Mid Yell now. There's the leisure centre, the school and the new surgery.' I got out of the car. 'I'll see you in a few hours. Have fun!'

It was difficult to concentrate on my clients' problems. My mind kept floating back to Liam and his future. The car was there to meet me when I finished work.

'What have you been up to?' I asked, as I settled into the back seat.

'We've been on a tour around the north of the island,' Rhys answered.

'Talking about options,' Liam added.

'Oh yes, good. And any conclusions?'

'I'm thinking about going back and sticking it out until the end of the year. See how I feel then. What do you think?'

'That sounds good. Even if you decide to leave then, at least you'll have a year's university education on your CV.'

'Yes, but it means I'll have to start revision. Exams are next week. It means leaving Shetland tomorrow.'

'So, when will you come back? I asked, looking into his green eyes, as we sat in the ferry terminal stretching the last few minutes out, not wanting to say goodbye.

'I don't know if I will be able to this year. You know what with work and everything.'

'How would you feel if we stayed here permanently?'

'It's up to you and Dad. There's nothing here for me. Obviously, I want you guys to be happy. I'll accept whatever you decide.'

What a wonderful young man. I'm so proud of you, Liam.

'Anyway, I wouldn't look right as a Viking,' he added stroking his 5oclock shadow. We all laughed but the time had come to part.

Don't cry, don't cry Janet!

We bear hugged and bear hugged again. We watched the baggy pants and the patterned Shetland hat bob down the corridor with attitude, turn at the ship's entrance, a last wide grin, a wave and he was gone. I looked at Rhys, his eyes watery and red. I grabbed his arm and we made our way back downstairs across the windy ferry terminal forecourt to the car. I looked back to see the Hrossey slowly pulling away on its journey down south.

When will see you again, son?

Viking Parade

Up Helly Aa, Lerwick

Viking helmets

Up Helly Aa, Scalloway

February 2005

The following weekend was time for Rachel. At Christmas, given how she was struggling without us there to support her through her PGCE, I had promised that we would try and see each other every two months or so. I found that I was due a day's leave for working New Year's Day so we arranged to meet in Edinburgh for a weekend in February. She would fly from Cardiff and I would get the North link ferry and the bus from Aberdeen.

It was a quiet crossing. I treated myself to a cabin for the first time and couldn't believe the luxury. It was like a night in a posh hotel - white fluffy towels, crisp sheets, comfortable bed, soft lighting- what a change from dossing down in the smoky lounge bar in a sleeping bag. I waited to see who my cabin companion would be, but as the evening wore on it looked like I was in luck and had the cabin to myself.

I retired early to enjoy the luxury and lay on the bed in the soft light, my thoughts drifting onto my relationship with our children. Liam's visit had made me realise something about myself; as a parent I was needy. I had to snatch every opportunity to be with our children and it seemed especially so as they were becoming independent. They still needed advice and support but I seemed to need them more centrally in my life. I needed them more than they needed me. It was a tricky balance between encouraging them to be self-reliant and keeping them close without smothering

them. I twirled my hair around my finger, looking at my distorted reflection in the glass of wine I had bought from the bar, looking for some sort of insight.
Hey, isn't this what drunks do, look for insight when they're in their cups? Snap out of it!

I also thought about Rhys. This would be the first time in five months or so that we had spent anytime apart. When we were at home in Wales I would often spend days out or the odd weekend with my women friends. I had thought that I might feel claustrophobic, just the two of us in Shetland. We had become closer, but I guess I did feel a bit claustrophobic, not just in our relationship but in my island life. I was really looking forward to having time with our daughter on my own.

Edinburgh is such a wonderfully elegant city. Up to then I had only seen the pavement from the airport bus stop as I pulled my bag behind me, concentrating on crossing Prince's Street, then walking up St Andrew's Street to the Bus Station and back again. On this occasion with more time to spare on arrival from Aberdeen, I spent the first few hours of Friday afternoon imbibing the city, the smell of traffic, the small green squares, the mixture of architecture and what seemed like vast crowds of people all hurrying purposefully somewhere to meet someone.

I had agreed to meet someone in a pub. Someone being an ex-colleague, Shane, a counsellor with the Royal College of Nursing. Shane is a young

Irish man from Tipperary, who had lived in Edinburgh for some years and had responsibility for delivering a service to nurse members across Scotland. We sat in the corner of a pub near the Haymarket, he with his pint and me with a gin and tonic. He got out his tobacco and started the comforting ritual I associated with him of rolling his own cigarette.

'So how are things at the RCN?' I asked.

'Don't ask,' he said. 'Still no news about whether the service is going to stay in-house or go out to tender. Bet you're glad you've moved on.'

'Yes I am, but I do miss the team-well, most of the team,' I smiled and Shane winked.

'Yes, *that* nameless woman is still a pain.'

'Has the team been back to the Moroccan restaurant off Oxford Street?'

'Yes, but it's not quite the same without you to share the pipe of peace with.'

'Go on with you. Though seeing Frida smoke apple sherbet through a hubble-bubble was quite something.' We both looked at each other through a tint of nostalgia and grinned. 'She may come up to visit.'
'That'll be fun. By the way, have I told you about my new venture?'

'No, what's that?'

'Myself and a friend are starting up an employee assistance programme. We're offering companies in Scotland consultancy, counselling and training. In fact, you could be our Shetland representative.'

'Sounds like Impact have got another competitor,' I laughed.

Impact is a company some friends and myself had set up several years ago to provide a similar service for companies in Wales. The small group had become close often socialising after meetings.

'Are you still involved with Impact?'

'Yes, but I've taken a sabbatical this year. If I stay in Shetland I'll have to resign from the Board.'

I felt quite nostalgic for meeting friends in city pubs. The fact that I rarely visited cities or pubs when I was home, seemed somewhat irrelevant. Then, suddenly a pretty young woman appeared at our table and introduced herself to Shane. I could tell he was impressed.

'I'm Rachel,' she said smiling and turned and gave me a big squeeze. We all sat and smiled at each other for a while.

'Let me get you a drink,' Shane asked. 'Same again,' he asked, pointing at my glass.

'Have you been to Shetland, Shane?' she asked, when he came back with the drinks.

'No, not yet Rachel.'

'Are you angling for an invite?' I laughed. 'I thought Shane didn't do rural and quiet. Well, you're invited anytime.'

'I had enough rural and quiet in Tipperary to last me a lifetime. Are you planning a visit, Rachel?'

'I hope to.'

'Well, your mother's e-mails make it sound an interesting enough place. She'd make a good Viking.'

'Can you recommend somewhere good to eat, Shane?' I said, changing the subject.

'There's a nice little Turkish place off Hanover Street.'

'Will you join us?'

'That's tempting, but my wife will be waiting for me. I'd better get back.' So we left Shane finishing his pint and we walked back up Princes Street towards Hanover Street.

We were staying with Chris and Barbara, friends who had moved to Edinburgh from Cardiff several years before. Chris had saved us in December, whisking Rhys and I off from the bus station to catch our flight home in time for Christmas.

By the time Rachel and I arrived at their home it was very late and we piled into their son's double bed, who was away at university in England. Sharing a bed with my daughter reminded me of the endless nights through my teenage years when I had to share a double bed with my mother. I hated it when my mother would cuddle up, like I was her husband. We had lived in a small two bedroomed flat and as I reached adolescence my parents thought it would be better to separate the sleeping arrangements for my younger brother and I. It meant that they would no longer sleep together. My relationship with my mother had been stormy and I never felt able to escape her. I was desperate for my own space. I noticed that Rachel kept well to her side of the bed. I wondered if there were issues around separation anxiety that had been there in my relationship with my mother and were now being played out in my relationship with my daughter. I made a note to talk to Freya, my art therapist about this when I next saw her.

Waking up early it was wonderful to hear garden bird song, something we missed in Shetland, where our garden was a lawn, a few windswept shrubs and the sound of seagulls squawking us out of bed. The smell of fresh coffee wafted through the house.

'Breakfast?' asked Barbara as we strolled into the kitchen.

Barbara was seated on a high stool reading the paper.

'The Saturday Guardian at 9.00am on Saturday.'

'When do you get to read it then?' asked Chris.

'Around 4pm, if we're lucky. Sometimes the magazine comes the following day. It's takes that long to reach the Co-op from the airport.'

'Oh, are those fresh croissants?' I asked.

'Yes, the joys of living right in the city. They're from the deli at the end of the street.'

'Don't. You're making me jealous. But, I guess you were always city people. Taff's Well was five miles too far out of Cardiff for you.'

'What are your plans?' Chris asked, as Rachel left the dining room and ascended the elegant Georgian staircase. 'Go on, have the last croissant, you poor deprived thing,' he said pointing at the object of my desire.

'Go out and see the sights, just spend some time with Rachel'

'We're going to the art cinema tonight, so if you fancy it, why not have dinner here first and then come along. I'll probably need to book.'

'Don't tell me, the cinema is also at the bottom of your street.'

'Not quite. Two blocks away.'

That day Rachel and I saw the sights, did the City bus tour, visited the new controversial Scottish Parliament building and ended up in the late afternoon drinking large glasses of shiraz, watching the Wales England Six Nations Rugby match in a busy pub. It was a great match. We cheered every time a Welsh player made a try much to the amusement of the Scottish and Irish crowd.

'They probably think we're drunk,' I tried to whisper.

'You mean, they probably think you're drunk,' she laughed.

This was something I wouldn't have ever done with Rhys as he breaks the stereotype of being Welsh and loving rugby.

'The two don't have to be synonymous,' he would say and regale me for the umpteenth time with the story of how before he was married, went on a rugby trip to Edinburgh with other teachers and while they were at the match he visited the art galleries.

I wouldn't normally have done this with Rachel either, who on home ground would not have wanted to be seen out in a local pub watching an international match with her mother, drunk or otherwise. I'm sure she would have called such a scenario 'sad.' Perhaps meeting on neutral territory was liberating for both of us.

In the evening after dinner and more wine, Chris and Barbara took us to their local cinema to watch a French film. They couldn't get tickets to the same film so at the entrance we parted.

'Here's a front door key,' said Chris, 'in case your film finishes before ours,'

After a few minutes in the warm atmosphere of the small cinema Rachel and I fell soundly asleep, coming to as the final credits played. I looked at a younger mirror image squinting back under smudged eye make-up.

'Do I look as bad as you?' I asked.

'You look worse,' came the sympathetic reply.

We got up and bleared our way back to Chris and Barbara's street. Rachel got to the door before me. She seemed to be having trouble opening it.

'Let me try,' I said, pulling the key from her hand, and poking it into the lock.

'Hey, what are you doing?' a voice shouted. We both shot up and looked over to see who it was.

'Our house is the next but one,' said Chris. 'I think a policeman lives at number 5.'

Early the following morning Chris took us to the bus station and we said our thank yous and goodbyes. Chris promised to come up to Shetland to see us later in the year. Rachel was going to meet up with a couple of friends before flying BMI Baby on the one hour trip back to Cardiff. I had a seventeen hour bus and ferry journey in front of me and then straight from the ferry on Monday morning into a seven hour counselling day. The week after next was half term and Rachel decided that, as she had plans for all her other school breaks, she would use this opportunity to come up to Shetland for a few days. It made saying farewell much easier.

While I had been gallivanting about in Edinburgh Rhys had re-discovered clubbing. He had been clubbing on three consecutive nights, something of a record for him. Thursday night had been Film Club, Friday night was Art Club and Saturday night, Bird Club. Somebody Rhys met thought his accent was Faeroese and invited him to join the Shetland-Faeroese Friendship Club. His clubbing possibilities were endless.

On February 8th 2005 Tracy returned to Shetland after the operation on her foot. She had been away longer than expected, a couple of months or more as I had predicted and I had missed her Bolton banter and her support as a colleague. She was limping slightly.

'Hello, Tiger. Dr P has been asking after you. He's looking forward to having you back.'

'Oh yes?'

'He has thirty new referrals he's been saving up especially.'

Tracy got hold of the nearest thing on the desk, a self-help guide on stress and beat me over the head with it. I pulled my hands up to protect my head.

'O.K. Tracy, I protested giggling. 'Welcome back.'

Two Sunday mornings later we arrived at the North Link ferry terminal at 7am to find Rachel looking bright and cheery after a full eleven hours sleep on the ferry from Aberdeen. I hadn't liked the thought of her dossing down on her own in the lounge bar of the Hrossey so I had booked her a cabin. It was also an enticement to do the long trip.

After a good breakfast we took her on the same tour as Liam and ended up at St Ninian's Isle, which is joined to the southern mainland at Bigton by a beautiful sandy tombolo. The light was often dramatic there, the low dunes streaked in shadow and illumination, pebbles standing on peaks of sand blown by Force 10 gales. Unfortunately, on this occasion it was raining. Also in deep winter, the sea on either sides of the sandy strip join forces and it is impossible to cross over to the island to see the 8th century chapel. This was the site of Pictish treasure, discovered during excavation in 1958 by a local schoolboy. The treasure consisted of 28 silver items, patterned brooches, bowls, a hanging lamp and a part of a porpoise jaw. They are now housed in the National Museum in Edinburgh with replicas in the Lerwick Museum.

'Do people swim here in the summer?' she asked miserably out of the rain splattered passenger side of the car.

'Yes, and even surf,' I said, hoping it might be a further enticement to return in the summer.

'Well, I won't be seeing that,' she said matter of factly.

I heard myself sigh.

'Shall we go on to Jarlshof?' Rhys asked, trying to interject some positivism in to the mood.

'What's there?' Rachel asked.

'A settlement, more than 2000 years old.' he replied.

'Oh, right.'

'You did history as part of your degree,' I stated in an effort to drum up some enthusiasm.

'That's not my period,' she said.

Great.

We arrived at Jarlshof. The rain hadn't subsided and we all looked at each other, not really wanting to get out of the car.

'I've done several drawings for the Bonhoga exhibition based on different aspects of the settlement,' Rhys said, trying to entice us out.

'You may never have another chance,' I urged.

'O.K. Let's go for it,' Rachel said, tumbled out of the car and ran towards the entrance at the edge of the sea.

In winter there was no-one manning the entrance so we gatecrashed to have a look around. The remains are complex and many layered through two and a half millennia of occupation. The site is dominated by the remains of a house with a tower dating from the late sixteenth century, built and extended by the infamous Stewart family, whose castle remains dominate the town of Scalloway. There are Bronze and Iron Age remains, including a broch or fort dating back to around 200BC and a number of wheelhouses built in a cluster in and around it. There is evidence of Pictish influence in the form of distinctive designs carved on stone. The Vikings' occupation of the settlement is believed to have started around 800 AD covering several centuries and remains of houses of stone and turf, that would have had wooden roof supports and a large central hearth lie at Jarlshof.

'Why is it called Jarlshof?' Rachel asked.

'Not sure, The Earl's house maybe? I think Walter Scott, the novelist gave it that name. Previously it was known as 'The auld hoose o' Sumburgh.'

'Come on, time for tea,' I said.

'That sounds nice. Is there a little café doing cream teas nearby?' she asked.

'fraid not. They all closed in September and won't be open until May. Tea will be at home. I've got some fresh smoked salmon though.'

'Sounds good. Let's go.'

The following day while I was working, Rhys gave Rachel the tour of Lerwick. In the late afternoon she went running around the sea loch and along the empty roads up to Califf and back to Strand Loch.

'The air is so pure. It's amazing. That was one of the best runs I've ever done,' she said, pulling off her muddy trainers in the hallway, her cheeks scarlet from the effort.

Rhys and I gave each other a secretive hopeful smile.

On her last night we decided to go to the weekly jam session of the Shetland Fiddle & Accordion Club held at the Asta Golf Clubhouse by Tingwall Loch. We had passed it on our fortnightly trips to the Film Club at Scalloway. We had first thought that it was someone's bungalow, with a big front room. We had thought how nice it was to see a family sitting around playing music together. Then someone told us it was the Golf Clubhouse and since then we had been dying to go along.

As we entered the 'front room', it was difficult to see anywhere to sit as the room must have held over

30 musicians, fiddlers, accordionists and guitarists cheek to jowl, engrossed in following each other's four by four rhythms. There were two piano players at either end of the room. One of the pianists, a lady in her eighties perhaps, never looked at the keys but held an on going conversation with those around her. Many of the men were large, red faced and sweating in their woollen Fair Isle pullovers. We caught sight of one woman playing what looked like a mobile harpsichord.

The front door kept opening and black music cases pushed their noses forward to find a little space where their owners could cosy up to the person next to them and play their instrument. We were the only people without an instrument and it wasn't the sort of music that you could sing along to. It was dance music but there was no space to dance and if there had been Rhys wouldn't have wanted to anyway. So we sat at the back to the side and tapped our feet and smiled encouragingly at the 50 odd musicians taking part. They were a friendly lot and in the break a couple asked us where we were from, while drinks were bought from the tiny bar in the corner. If we had played an instrument it would have been a great way of getting to know people and have fun. No home bakes this time though, so after an hour or so we left our heads full of Boston two steps but our stomachs empty.

Later that night as we stuffed ourselves yet again with smoked salmon, I asked Rachel what she thought of Shetland.

'Well, it's dramatic but there's nothing much here for young people that I've seen. It's so far from anywhere and such a trek to get here.'

'Would you come back?'

'Yes, I'd like to see what it's like in the summer if I can, but I don't know what I'll be doing yet, so I can't promise.'

The following evening we took her down to the ferry. We hugged goodbye. She smelt of fresh air and coconut shampoo. We watched her drag her pull-along case down the covered gangplank, she didn't look back and disappeared into the ship.

'God, this hello-goodbye malarkey is hard work.'

Rhys nodded and not for the first time I caught a glimpse of his grey blue eyes watering over.

When we got back to the house I needed some distraction so set to washing and ironing Rachel's bedclothes. I held the pillowcase to my face. There was a faint smell of her Dolce & Gabbana perfume. I sat on the bed and thought, what else is this feeling of loss about? Hanging out with my daughter who was more like a friend, had given me that feeling of a remembered youth that was fun, exciting and unpredictable. I ripped off the sheets and thrust them into the washing machine.

It was now nearing the end of February. The days were getting a bit longer and from our picture window in Strand Loch we saw oystercatchers and swans and heard curlews calling each other in their piercing dialect. It was my day for visiting Yell. It had snowed again, was sunny and bright and I had an excellent crossing. The air was so clean and intoxicating. There was a Beatles song aptly playing on the ferry, 'In my life'. I should have felt on top of the world but I felt low and unsettled. I decided to have an art therapy session with Freya to see if together we could make any sense of what I was feeling.

'After that first time in hospital when you were little, did you ever feel abandoned again?' Freya asked, when we met later that week in her studio.

'Yes, I suppose to some degree after my brother was born and I was no longer the absolute centre of my parents' attention. But more so, when I was a teenager.'

'Tell me about it,' she said.

'My mother had chest problems, due to heavy smoking, and in two consecutive winters she got pneumonia, then she was diagnosed with lung cancer around the time I was taking my finals at college. It was pitiful to see her, she got smaller and smaller.'

'Would you like to paint?'

I took up my paintbrush and attempted to paint. There was a large ugly bird, with wings somewhat outstretched, bulging eyes and a very sad expression.

'I had to continue to sleep with her in my parents' double bed throughout her illness. Lung cancer is horrific. She constantly coughed up litres of white fluid. I felt helpless. She only lasted for about five months after her diagnosis.'

'What was that like for you?'

'I don't remember if I cried at her funeral, but I howled beneath the eiderdown for weeks afterwards. I felt she had abandoned me. I don't remember crying for her after I left for Indonesia a couple of months later. In fact, I rarely cry.'

'Can you relate any of that to how you're feeling now?'

'Yes. I feel that I have abandoned my own daughter by moving away at the time she needed me most. But, I also feel somewhat lost, like an outsider.'

I had felt this at many points in my life. To some extent it had suited me. Being an outsider means you can observe the world without opening up your own vulnerabilities, without committing to one group or another. You can be anonymous. On the downside nobody may care much about you. You hear these stories of elderly people being found on their own, dead for days and nobody knowing. It's difficult to imagine that ever happening in Shetland. In a small community that relies on your energy and participation to make it work effectively, there's no possibility of being anonymous. But perhaps you could feel stifled and trapped by the interest of others. I realized that what I longed for and what I was looking for, wherever I had been living in this country or abroad, was a sense of belonging and purpose. Belonging to what I still didn't know.

The 27th of February 2005 was a great day for Wales. In the Six Nations rugby tournament Wales beat France 21-15. 'Thrilling', 'breath taking', 'magnificent' were words used by TV commentators to describe Wales performance. I sat in the blue armchair in the lounge, wearing my red and green Wales scarf, screeching like a banshee at every attempt for a try. I had never got to see a match at the Arms Park or the new Millennium Stadium and after all these years I still didn't know all the words to the national anthem, but as I sat watching the match I carried on another conversation with myself.

Is it Wales that pulls your heartstrings? Is it Wales where I belong? Get real, woman! Can an English woman ever belong to Wales?

An English accent pigeonhole's you, stamps you with an imagined identity. People make assumptions about you. In the south my estuary accent betrays my working class background. In the South Wales valleys I've been called posh. When I support Wales on the rugby field my brother reminds me where I've come from.

Does accident of birth condemn you to a straight-jacket of identity in other people's minds?

To belong to a society like Shetland you would have to be here for the long haul. You would have to contribute and participate. Would you still be an outsider?

I guess in coming to Shetland initially I hadn't set out to belong, just to experience something different from our life in Wales. We were certainly doing that, but...
Would it be a case of once a soothmoother, always one?

St Ninian's Isle

Papil, Winter

March 2005

St David's Day had been odd. Rhys went out looking for daffodils. There were none on sale in the flower shop because the order hadn't arrived on time. I did contemplate stealing a few from the neighbour's garden but it would have been pretty pointless as they were hardly recognizable, just small green shoots in the soil. Shetland was way behind in spring flower growth compared with the south. They reckoned that 2005's spring was about a month behind England and Wales.

In the first few days of March the weather was foul, wind, rain, sleet, snow, then suddenly the mist raised itself from the low hills opposite Strand Loch, the skies cleared and the world was calm again.

'Let's get out,' Rhys said. 'I've got to have some fresh air. What about walking down to Califf and back across the moorland behind the house. We haven't done that yet.'

We wrapped up warm as usual with several layers, waterproofs just in case, boots, gloves, camera, our usual picnic in our rucksack. To look at us you would have thought we were going on a 20mile hike rather that than the two miles to Califf and two back. We walked along the road until we reached the sea and then started the gentle climb up into the moorland. I was always the slow one then, and Rhys was some way ahead when I noticed he had stopped and I caught his profile looking very excited. He turned, waving and sshing me to stop.

'Ahead, to the right, a white hare,' he mouthed.

My eye travelled along the line of his pointed finger and then I saw it, snowy white with a silvery back standing pert high on its back legs watching us both intently with its albino eyes. Hares camouflage themselves in winter and now against the dark moor land we were lucky enough to get our first sighting.

'Look again, higher up.'

There, further up, his mate sat frozen to the spot, given away by two long white ears above the parapet of springy blackened heather.

'Damn, I've forgotten the binoculars,' he said while trying to extricate the camera without taking his eyes off these splendid creatures. Then in a blink they disappeared.

'Let's try and follow them.' Rhys cried, as he leapt over the heather, with me trying to keep up. As we reached the top and looked down towards our house, we caught another couple of sightings of white silvery fur stop and start across the moor.

'Breath taking!' I exclaimed.

As if that wasn't enough excitement for one day, as we sloped down towards Strand Loch we felt we were audience to the most exuberant stage set. Two families of mute and whooper swans glided across the water against a backdrop of striped peach and turquoise sky. In front, more than a hundred grey lag geese could be seen, pecking their way in lines across the grassy field like policemen on a forensic search.

The day had been perfect. My spirits had been lifted by the wonder world of Shetland's nature and the strong connection I felt to the land, the sky, the sea, the elements, my husband and to other species co-habiting in close proximity. As we sat in the lounge, watching the last light of the day disappear I said,

'Perhaps, at some level this is really what belonging means to me, a kind of oneness with the universe. Maybe I belong nowhere in particular but everywhere in essence. Sounds awful cheesy, doesn't it?'

'Yes, but I feel it too. You could call it a spiritual experience,' Rhys said, looking out at the few car headlights criss-crossing down the slalom from the Westside. As he slowly drew the curtains on the outside world I got even more profound.

'I wonder if the desire to connect with others, to the environment, to the weather and to nature is a fundamental human need that paradoxically can only be met in death. You know, dust to dust and all that.'

'That's deep and depressing,' my husband muttered. 'What's on the box tonight? I feel like a laugh.'

The following day was Mother's Day. I managed to have a row with Liam because his card hadn't arrived. *What a brat I can be.* We made it up over a text or two. Rachel sent me a book called 'Sea Room' by Adam Nicolson about life on three islands off Lewis in the Outer Hebrides and a sea green necklace. Rhys spoilt me with breakfast in bed and a roast beef supper. We amused each other by trying to guess each other's bird sounds. *What we do for entertainment, eh?* I hadn't been looking forward to the day without the children but it turned out fine and I was starting to feel a bit brighter.

March marched on. The weather continued to be wintery, snow, sleet showers with the occasional bright spot. Rhys had been busy all winter preparing his exhibition and it was now ready to start its travels at Sumburgh airport on a journey that would take it to the walls of several island community centres.

Rhys' 'thing', his passion, is trees, particularly roots, gnarled, dancing over rocks, spreading themselves out across the surface of the earth, their fingers clinging on in their attempts to find sustenance and life. *There could just be a metaphor in* there *somewhere.* The problem for him in coming to Shetland was that there aren't many trees and those that exist are the dwarf stumpy variety that don't have quite the same appeal. Rhys uses mainly pastels and coloured inks and considering he trained as a stained glass artist and lithographer his pictures are often very dark and mysterious. His work expresses to him the essence of being Celtic, rooted in life forces, the very nature, power and mysteries of the ancient landscape, its decay and regeneration. This identity plays an important part in his creative response to the life and landscape of different worlds. I keep urging him to lighten them up as most people don't seem to want to live with the forces of darkness on their living room walls.

He isn't that inspired by the sea to the same extent so on arrival he looked around for other interesting subject material and his creative eye fell on ancient stones, visual impressions of ancient architecture. Our weekends were spent searching them out, many in remote locations and others only accessible in the summer. He took lots of photos as sketching in Shetland winds became frustrating. I got fed up stumbling over peat and heather to retrieve his embryonic masterpieces. We also lost a lot because I don't run very fast. His weekdays were spent in our utility room, his makeshift studio. His drawing board perched on the fridge freezer, with warmth from the boiler and Radio Shetland his only companion, he had spent a productive winter and now his efforts were to be on show. Considering we had been in Shetland for such a short time it was quite an achievement. I don't think I could have been that self-motivated working in such solitariness.

The other great thing about the subject matter was that nobody else was painting and drawing the ancient monuments. Most painters looked to the sea because the point where North Sea meets Atlantic Ocean is just so exciting. The luminous qualities of light and water provide a dramatic landscape enjoyed and re-created on canvas by many local and visiting artists. The Archaeology Department of Shetland Islands Council was encouraging and even seemed interested in having postcards published. They bought a few small pictures for their Iron Age Village shop but we don't know if the post cards materialized. Although the Shetland Islands Council and Arts Trust encourage the arts, what we came to realize was that they are not so successful at promoting the travelling exhibitions and any publicity has to be done primarily by the artist.

'Doesn't look too bad, does it?,' Rhys asked me, as we stood gazing at the row of glowing visual remains of Shetland's past hung in black frames on white walls that are used as an exhibition space in Sumburgh's tiny airport.

'I'm calling it 'Turning Point'. It represents a change of direction, of difference in my work and a growing interest in the relationship between the Norse, the Picts and the Celts. What do you think?'

'I like it. It could also represent this change of direction in our own lives. But, don't be so modest. It looks bloody brilliant. I'm really proud of you. Now, let's hope others like it and want to buy. Come on, let's go and celebrate.'

On Monday 21st of March we looked out of the kitchen window to see the brown hills to the Westside transformed into sparkling white pavlovas waiting to be devoured.

'I'll come in with you this morning. I want to go into a couple of galleries,' Rhys said, as I applied mascara to my puffy morning eyes. I looked out of the bedroom window at the polar stillness and back into the room. I wouldn't be needing hairspray. I had never been one for hairspray, well not since the 1960's when I plastered it on my bouffant like every other sixteen year old. It was different then, it smelt foul and you could see and feel the chemicals looking like white splattered mist over a backcombed beehive. Shetland changed all that. I soon realized that if I wanted to retain any lift on my thinning shorter crop it was no use spending time in rollers, because at the very moment of opening the door, the wind played her merry game of mess up and even before I got into the car, my highlighted mop had spread across my face. It looked like I hadn't even bothered combing my hair before coming out, and of course removed any trace of a lift. It was hairspray or a hat. A hat flattens, hairspray immobilises; so on workdays hairspray usually won. But, on this Monday my hair welcomed a hairspray-free day.

Rhys brushed the heavy snow off the car windscreen. We smiled at each other. The sky spangled in the winter sun. He knew better than to throw a snowball. When I'm geared up for work I don't do fun.

'Bendigedig, Wonderful!' he said.

'Yes, isn't it. Do you mind driving?'

'No problem,' he said and jumped into the driver's seat.

We drove out of the cul de sac with open mouths. I felt a cliché coming on, but Rhys swerved to avoid it. We moved onto the road.

'How beautiful. Look at the long shadows on the drift.'

'Wow! said Rhys, turning his head in the direction of art. At that perfect moment my mind registered that there weren't any tyre marks on the snow in front of us and immediately we came to a halt, the car wheels stuck in the freshness of the drift. No one else had been this stupid.

'I'm going to be late for work,' I said, noticing my tendency to say unhelpful things in moments of crisis. 'Nothing for it, I'll have to walk to the main road and then I'll get a bus.'

Rhys revved up and the wheels spun like the London Eye on speed. I noted Rhys' tendency to plough the same field in moments of crisis and consequently dig himself into deeper mess. Except, on this occasion we weren't in a field but we were close to one. We got out of the car. We looked at the car half sunk in snow and shook our heads. We were well and truly stuck. I took my Wellington boots out of the back and found an old hat of Rhys'. My clients would just have to see me as a flat head today.

'I'll catch you up,' he said.

As I pushed my wee legs against the weight of the snow and towards my goal, the main road about half a mile away, I imagined myself a polar explorer and at the same time noted my natural sense of drama in any crisis. Well, it was probably as close as I'd want to get to the Arctic anyway. I turned to see Rhys sitting back in the driver's seat frowning and puzzling. He has a tendency to pull the dewlap of skin under his chin when he's anxious and it was having a good tug. I just knew he was asking himself how the hell we'd landed up in a snowdrift.

As I pushed up the lane a smiling red-faced man in rubber dungarees carrying a spade approached.

'We saw you struggling from our window,' he smiled, pointing to his house overlooking the Loch to the south side.

'It looks like he could do with a hand.'

'Oh thank you. He certainly could.'

I continued walking up to the main road. Cars were driving at walking speed, slip sliding across the brow of the hill towards Lerwick. As I stepped onto a passing bus, I peered out of the steamy window. I could see our saviour shaking Rhys hand and the two of them laughing.

When I finally reached work there were several messages from clients who couldn't get into the surgery because of the weather conditions. My day looked refreshingly empty.

'Most people don't even try to get in,' said the receptionist at Lerwick Health Centre. 'It's too difficult. Last year some roads on Westside were impassable for three days. 'You have to make sure your freezer is well stocked up at this time of the year and have plenty of electricity coupons if you're on the meter. Oh, and don't forget to have spade and a blanket in the boot, just in case.'

As the day went on the snow began to melt and I managed to get an early bus home. The snow ploughs had been working on the B roads and so Rhys was able to come and meet me at the T junction.

'Did the guy berate you and tell you what silly Soothmoothers we were?'

'No, he was very polite and helpful, but I can't help feeling he was thinking it.'

By the following day the snow had been cleared from the main roads and I was able to get into Lerwick for my early morning art therapy session before heading off for the ferry to Whalsay. We decided to do a review of the work to date. We looked at my mission to find my true self and explored what that might look like.

'If you were the weather, what would you be?' Freya asked, cradling her first coffee of the day in her sculptor's hands.

Ooh, I like that. I must use that one with my clients.

She had a tendency to sit with her palms outward when she was listening intently to me. With her wet hair pulled back into a ponytail she reminded me of a benevolent earth Buddha. I felt total acceptance.

'I'd be dramatic, exhilarating, fearful, harsh, cold, warm, exciting, sensational.'

What do you make of that then, Freya!

The man in the Rod and Line shop had been quite clear.

'When you arrive at Fetlar, look out for the nuns of St Agnes. They are often at the quay to welcome strong men,' he told Rhys, when he popped into the shop for advice on fishing tackle.

'I've been spotted a couple of times when I've gone over to watch the red-necked phalarope. Before you know it they have you working in their community garden and you'll be greetin' (sobbing) on the tatties for the rest of your day.'

Trying to hide when you are one of just three cars arriving on the small ferry is difficult so we looked into the middle distance as we drove off the boat, hoping that greeting would not turn to greetin' on our first weekend away on a distant isle.

Fetlar, a northern isle east of Yell, and had been described to us as the 'Garden of Shetland' on account of its fertile soil. The geology is mostly serpentine, supporting a flora of grassland rich in wild flowers. However, although this time of year sees the start of spring down south, here it would be unlikely that you would see wildflowers until June. We had come to see the birds, especially the rare migrant to Shetland, the red-necked phalarope, do some walking and exploring. Rhys was also keen to continue his search for ancient stones.

The Hjaltadans is a ring of large stones surrounding a shallow ditch, with two larger stones at the centre and may date from the Bronze Age. The centre stones are said to be a fiddler and his wife who were surprised by the dawn which turned them and the dancing trows (trolls) to stone as the sun rose. The island had a population of 761 in 1842 but the owner decided that sheep were better than people and soon cleared most off the island, using croft house and broch stones to build his now decaying folly. Sadly, the population never recovered.

Fetlar's greatest claim to fame in the natural world was the Snowy Owl, which bred here between 1967 to 1975, but our main goal was to see the red-necked phalarope so we dumped our stuff at the B & B and set off in search of them.

We did our first reconnaissance by car to get the feel of the place. In Shetland it is road etiquette to raise the index finger of your right hand off the steering wheel and point at whatever you pass; other drivers, animal, vegetable or mineral. It gives you the sense of having a wide social network. Not to be confused with the inverted middle finger, which would give you a reduced one. On Fetlar, our fellow travellers clearly were not aware of this rule as the driver and passengers in the other two cars set their jaws and studiously ignored us. After you've passed each other back and forth several times on the only stretch of road that runs the six mile length of the island you either get jaw ache or give in and smile.

As we reached the Loch of Funzie, a small stretch of water sparkling in the winter sun, a flock of tiny dunlins pitter-pattered away at speed, and a few large birds sought flight against our intrusion.

'There's the hide, over there,' I pointed across the Loch.

'Great, let's go.' said Rhys, salivating at the thought of seeing a rare bird.

We walked around the edge of the loch. The hide door was stiff to open. It should have been a clue. We settled down, our binoculars stuck to our faces and surveyed the hidden water in front of the reed beds.

'Can you see one, Rhys?'

'No, not yet. Look over there, those brown birds with long red legs, they're Redshanks.'

'What should signs should I be looking out for?'

'A white throat, a fine black bill, the female has a blackhead, the male reddish brown; both sexes have dark slate-grey upper parts, and obviously red necks. They also have a white wing-bar in flight. They are fast fliers so you really have to watch carefully, otherwise you'll miss them.'

Having been brought up in London and not really discovering nature until I came to live in Wales, I always felt a novice when out with Rhys. He was brought up overlooking the Tregaron bog in mid Wales, the oldest bog in Europe. As a child he had sat on his grandmother's shoulders using the telescope his grandfather had used in Klondike in the 1890's, to watch and name birds on the bog. So I viewed him as an expert in all things green and brown.

We sat for some time peering out, with me repeating, 'Have you seen one yet, Rhys?' and him patiently repeating, 'Sssh, no not yet.' It was already past lunchtime and I was getting fidgety.

'What about some lunch? I think the shop closes in the afternoons. We'll need to go soon if we want to eat before supper.'

The B&B has a fine reputation for its home cooking, but supper was five hours away. Rhys took the binoculars away from his face slowly and with his neck still strained in the direction of the reed beds, looked wistful as he stepped over the bench and pulled the wooden door letting us out into the sunshine.

'Perhaps we'll see one later,' I said encouragingly.

That evening in the warmth of the dining room at the B & B, Rhys talked about his disappointment in not seeing the rare red-necked phalarope. He was overheard by the landlord, who interrupted,

'You'll not see a phalarope at this time of year. You'll have to come back in June. That's when you'll see them breeding here in Fetlar.'

Silly Soothmoothers, yet again. So much for my wildlife expert. I'll read the bird book myself next time.

It had been a great weekend though and we came home refreshed and ready for the week. Rhys's disclosure form had come back from the Criminal

Records Bureau. It is a requirement to have a clean record with no criminal convictions if you're working with children or vulnerable adults. He had been through many of these checks in Wales. Every organization he worked for as a supply teacher required one. It is costly and time consuming and goodness knows why you can't use the same record for each organization, but you can't. In being checked out by the Shetland Education Authority he even had to give details of his teacher training course, some forty odd years ago, despite having taught in Wales at a senior level for most of that time. This together with the police checks had meant that it had taken almost four months before he was able to make himself available for supply teaching in Shetland.

Rhys set off earlyish for Whalsay on his first supply teaching assignment to be sure of getting the ferry on time. At home he had a tendency to push time to its very limits, allowing no margin of error or a large vehicle on the road and usually the last to creep into the pre-assembly teachers' meeting, triumphant that he'd proved yet again that he was punctual - just. This had been a tension in our marriage as I was brought up by a bus inspector father, who measured time in milliseconds and to be late was a cardinal sin. I found holding on to the anxiety of being late too much to bear and sometimes this fear would get acted out in a drama resembling the eruption of Krakatoa. That morning I

could feel the tension rise in me as I saw him dash for the car, tugging on his dewlap. I closed the front door.
I wonder if he remembered to book the ferry? Don't think about black ice. Get on with your day.

'I managed to get the ferry,' he told me that evening, as we sat down to eat and he reported on the events of his day. 'No, I didn't book,' he added before I asked.

'Tell me all,' I said, and he continued,

'As I sat down with my coffee, I heard a whirring noise, a jolt and then silence.

'Oh no,' I thought. 'I'm going to be late on my first day. I made my way down to the car on the open deck'

'What's happening?' I asked a crew member's backside as he and several others folded themselves over the side to see what was wrong.

'Braken doon. Dunna worry. We'll get a tow from the another ferry. 'Shouldn't tack more than an hour.'

'That's awful dialect Rhys, but carry on.' I interrupted.

'An hour? I thought these ferries are spanking new.' I said to the man.

'They are,' he said, 'but they are having their teething problems.' He said that they are difficult to turn around at the dockside and take more time to do so than the older ferries.

'Yes, that's what Emily told us. Sorry, go on.'

'Relax, there's nothing you can do, he told me, 'so why not grab another coffee and keep in the warm.'

'Suddenly, I heard a whirring noise and saw a red spot in the distance getting larger and louder,' Rhys said, getting into his adventure.

'It's the cavalry!' said the crew member. Then he told me that it was the sea and air rescue helicopter based at Sumburgh. He said that it was probably oot on training. I looked up and waved at what looked like a red bird hovering over the boat.

'What? The red-necked phalarope at last!'

'It didn't have a black head, but it did have a white wingbar,' Rhys laughed. Then the man said,

'This may be your lucky day. How do you fancy being airlifted off?'

'And what did you say?' I asked, putting a forkful of pasta into my mouth.

'I'd rather not. I can't swim.'

'Only joking,' the man replied and then he asked me what I was doing on Whalsay. I was in the middle of explaining when, from behind, I thought I heard my name carried on the wind. I turned and a gentleman in a suit and a mop of black windswept hair approached wishing me good morning.

'Who was it?' I asked. 'Hey, this is delicious. Is there any more?'

'Yes, I'll get some now. Can I finish the story? It was the headmaster. I told him I was worried that I was going to be late, but he said,'

'Yes, it's a nuisance, but look towards the island and up at the large building on the hill. That's the school. Did you see that glint in the sun? ' he asked me. 'That's the school secretary with the binoculars. She can see what's happened. I'm sure my deputy will be taking assembly as we speak.'

We both laughed.

'Quite an adventure for a first day then? What was the school like?'

'It was nice. The staff were friendly. I took a number of junior classes for art.'

'Great! I bet you enjoyed the little ones. Now, what about seconds?'

The following week Rhys got a call from a school in Brae, a large village about twenty miles from where we lived. This was a new community school, its sports and leisure facilities built like the others across Shetland with revenue from the oil terminal at Sullom Voe not far away. On this occasion Rhys caught the early morning bus. That evening after dinner we had another debrief.

'I met that man from the Althing Debating Club on the bus.'

'Which man was that?' I asked, sitting myself down on the sofa ready to hear about his day.

'The one who spoke so well in the debate about the war in Iraq.'

'Oh yes, I know the one. In his thirties?'

'Yes, that's the one. He invited me to sit by him. He is a history teacher at Brae and when he found out that I was Welsh he asked lots of questions at about bilingualism and Welsh nationalism. Nice chap.'

'Good. So what was the school like?'

'Well, when I arrived at the school I was directed to a classroom. Sitting at the desk at the front was a large chap with a full Blackbeard face.'

'Yes?'

'I thought the beard must be a leftover from Up-Helly-Aa. When I first started teaching, teachers were not allowed to have beards.'

'Really?'

'Excuse me,' I said, 'I am the new supply teacher, Ieuan Rhys Daniel,' and I lent forward to shake the man's hand.

'Yes?'

'He said, 'The teacher will be here shortly.'

'Right?'

'I said, 'Oh, fine. I will wait.' Then I asked him if he had been teaching at the school for long.' 'Teaching?' he said. 'I'm not a teacher, I'm a pupil.'

I burst out laughing.

'I was so embarrassed. Then I realized that this was the pupil I would be working with on a one to one basis for the rest of the day. When Blackbeard stood up he towered over me and said, 'I'm supposed to have a swimming lesson.''

'Oh no! You can't swim.'

'That's exactly what I told the school secretary.'

'So what happened?'

'She said not to worry and that I could supervise him in the gym instead!'

Over the next few months Rhys did supply teaching in a number of secondary schools across Shetland and found himself covering for subjects he knew little or nothing about, such as German, IT and Maths. Where teachers hadn't left any work he managed by finding a creative or artistic angle on the subject. How you would make a poster on an algebraic problem I have no idea, but the feedback was usually positive. He also did supply in primary schools, where he only taught art. He loved working with the younger children, he enjoyed their spontaneity and originality and he always came home in a buoyant mood.

Whalsay Ferry

April 2005

On Saturday the 2nd of April it was very warm and sunny and I found myself wearing a short-sleeved blouse. The clocks had gone forward the previous weekend and it wasn't dark until 9pm. I had more energy and felt in a better mood.

Tracy had invited the team and their partners to lunch at her new rented house just up the road. Her partner Valerie was up from the south and together they had put on a big spread. Gerrie had brought their grandchildren, and Joe, her husband played happily on the floor with the small boys and Tracy's collection of toy tigers.

Emily and Donald had come down from Unst and as usual Donald and Calum sat engrossed in each other's company talking about science. It was difficult to get a word in but opportunities to talk to Donald were rare so I persevered. Donald was a social activist. He and Emily had spent time working in the Sudan, Ethiopia and Nepal. Donald worked as a consultant for Save the Children and was about to go out to Indonesia in connection with post Tsunami development. I had spent three years working there in my early twenties so there was a lot to share. Donald also ran an alternative energy project, involving the development of hydrogen, produced through wind energy as a potential source of fuel for cars. He wasn't paid for much of his work on Unst, but his commitment to regeneration and a principled way of living meant that he spent most of his time working.

The sun blazed through the large picture window and we sat chatting and laughing. I looked around at my colleagues and thought how lucky I had been to meet and work with such a great bunch of caring, committed and interesting people. It was going to be very hard to tell them that Rhys and I were seriously considering returning home at the end of our first year. We had agonized over our dilemma, having endless late night conversations asking ourselves, 'Should we stay or should we go?' I had mentioned how I was feeling to Calum but asked him to keep it confidential. We hadn't quite reached a decision but it was looking possible.

We decided not to say anything until we came back after a short break home over Easter. We were still not sure, but I didn't want people to disconnect from us, to withdraw, which is what often happens when loss is forewarned. It's a natural human defence. Why continue to get attached and closer to someone who is going to shortly abandon you? Maybe that was selfish but I also knew that I would struggle with the pain of loss of such good colleagues and friends, so best to try and make the most of every moment.

We were warned that the weather might be very bad when we set off once more on the 20hour journey down south and that we might miss the tide in Aberdeen, with the result of missing our bus and flight connections. As these were of the cheapo variety, if you missed them you lost them and you would just have to fork out another £xx for the next ones. I called Rachel and asked her to change our flights if it cost no more than £20 each, just to be on the safe side. Rhys and I tucked ourselves into our sleeping bags in a less smoky part of the lounge bar and hoped for the best.

We awoke to a bright Aberdeen morning. The crossing had been fine and we'd arrived on time, but then we faced waiting in Edinburgh airport to the late evening, when the changed flight took off adding several more hours to the journey. So much for my forward thinking.

We were only home for a few days but it was wonderful to be home. Rachel and I had fun going shopping. We saw family and friends. We pottered in the garden and I did a couple of trips up to mid Wales to see two of my closest friends. It was strange yet normal. When we were home it was as if our Shetland life didn't exist and when Rhys and I were in Shetland it was often difficult to remember what life was like at home, but somehow we both yearned for it. Everywhere new green and lush growth was emerging. Daffodils marched their way along the verges of the dual carriageways in all directions but Cardiff seemed claustrophobic, busy and polluted.

On the day before we were due to go back Liam showed up from a snowboarding trip in Switzerland. It was a very happy family reunion and we went out to a

Greek restaurant to celebrate. Saying goodbye was as difficult as usual. As the taxi taking us to our early morning flight picked up speed I glanced over my shoulder at the still house and looked at Rhys who was tugging his dewlap.

'I am not sure I can keep doing this,' I muttered.

'I agree, so what shall we do? 'he replied mournfully.

I've come back in order to go home. Does that make any sense?' I told the gang at the Monday morning team meeting.

It was Gerrie's last day. Working as a part-time counsellor in two services was exhausting and she had decided to finish her work with the primary care counselling service in order to work full-time for the alcohol advice & support service. I hadn't wanted to steal her thunder, and I blurted out my news, while she had popped out to the loo, without properly thinking through the impact that both of us going would have on the small close knit team.

'It's like the Paul Coelho story, 'The Alchemist,' I told them. 'A young shepherd boy leaves his village to explore the world beyond the sea that divides Europe from North Africa. He has many adventures but only finds the treasure he is searching for when he eventually gets back home. It was there under the ground of the shady olive tree that before his travels he had come to despise for its familiarity. I feel that I came to Shetland and have rediscovered what is important to me in life. I also feel just too far away from my children.'

'If you've come to Shetland to find your true self and found it, that's fine, because you've also made a contribution to our work,' said Calum, his eyes glistening. The rest of the team looked somewhat dazed but muttered nice things.

'I would prefer not to talk about it, if that's ok,' I said. 'It's still a long way off to September and I want to concentrate on making the most of the rest of the time with you.' They all nodded sagely.

'What have I missed?' said Gerrie, coming back into the room smiling in the euphoria of her last day.

'Quite a bit, Gerrie. I'll tell you at coffee,' I said. 'What's the agenda today, Calum?'

Gerrie wanted to go to Monty's for her leaving do. Having been a chef for many years she was fussy where she ate. She appreciated good food and was prepared to pay for it. The rest of the team also appreciated good food but some of the English didn't want to spend as much as we knew a meal would cost there, especially as we would be paying for her meal too. It was rather mean as Gerrie like most Shetlanders is a very generous person. Anyway, we invited her to Raba, a Bangladeshi restaurant opposite the Viking bus station in Lerwick and we had a nice if not heavy meal but a jolly evening all the same.

That night I paid for my meanness as I found it difficult to get to sleep. The Tandoori sat beneath my rib cage like a mountain of slate. I also had my clients in the marital bed and I tossed and turned their problems over and over again. Their faces kept appearing, and when I turned one way, there was another face on the other side looking sad and wanting. People often ask me, 'How do you turn off after a day of listening to such depressing stories?' I didn't usually have a problem. I took any issues that were causing me difficulties to supervision or talked them over with colleagues, especially Calum, who was always ready to listen.

But that night I couldn't switch off. I had had a heavy day. Then joining the clients in our marital domain were the doctors. In the Lerwick practice the GPs were immensely busy. The waiting list for referrals to the counselling service was growing. I felt I was making a contribution and feedback from clients was positive but the doctors' total lack of interest in me as a person was raising its head again, accentuating my feeling of being an outsider and invisible. I kicked the duvet off my legs. Is it a doctor thing? Are they are too wrapped up in the care of their patients to have time to care for their colleagues? I hadn't expected doctors down south to show interest in me, so why here? Or is it a generation thing? I was the eldest professional in the practice apart from the practice manager. Isn't this what older women often feel, wherever they live? Invisible.

I hauled the 20togs over to my side of the bed. 'Invisible,' is what it had said on a middle aged client's

T shirt, with the letters fading so you had to get really close to read it. Something she might have been quite pleased about if the person was male, young and good looking but it probably wouldn't have been. More likely to be another radical feminist who she wouldn't necessarily have wanted too close to her chest. I rubbed the slate mountain. Would they have been more interested if I was younger?

I looked at younger colleagues in the practice, who were solitary workers and in speaking to them I realized that they also often felt invisible in that practice. They're busy people with their own families. I guess if I had my family here, old friends and a more active social life this wouldn't be such an issue for me. Or was I just an irritating attention seeker? If I wasn't going to say something I might regret I just had to accept the situation. I got up and went to the bathroom.

'Have we got any Rennies?' I burped, as I rummaged through the cabinet.

Before Raba I had also been on the phone talking to Rachel, who was finding teaching practice in her second school very difficult. It wasn't the children but her mentor's lack of experience and guidance. She seemed to be in a very negative place and I was worried that she was becoming depressed. Too many classes and an impossible workload for a trainee. She was scraping the barrel in asking for my advice as I had never taught English to children, but it didn't stop me trying. I really wanted to be near, to make it alright. But

I couldn't, so I phoned Liam to hear that he was finding it weird being back in university after the Easter hols in Switzerland. I just hoped he would stick it out.

I was looking forward to talking things over with Freya. She was in the process of moving from her studio in the Lanes to a room in the new building of the council for voluntary organisations. I arrived early to find her at the door waiting for me.

'You won't believe this. They took my wood,' said Freya, as I followed her in.

'Who did?' I said trying to look suitably askance, but not having a clue as to what she meant.

'The Voar Redd Up.'

At the end of April there was a big environmental event in Shetland, called 'Voar Redd Up'. Schools, voluntary organisations and individuals take part in a big clean up. Bags of rubbish collected from the beaches during the winter gales stand like stumpy lumpy soldiers on the roadside waiting to be transported to the dump. Freya was something of a beachcomber, regularly collecting and hiding wood that might be useful for the fire or as sculptural objects of art needing a place in her garden. Her favourite place for beachcombing was Bannaminn near Papil on Burra Isle. She had stacked her driftwood neatly by the side of the beach. That weekend Rhys and I had been down to the wonderful turquoise paradise for a stroll and noticed how clean it was looking.

'Anyway, how was your week?' she said handing me a hot cup of coffee.

'I saw a lamb born, I fell off my bike and I went to the Book Club.'

'Are the events connected?'

'Probably, but I'm not sure how yet.'

'Tell me all about it,' she said settling into her comfy chair and opening her palms, the sign I had her full attention.

I often wished that Freya was my friend and not my therapist. I felt we'd have a lot in common. But professional ethics held us back. I also knew that some of my clients wanted to be my friend, but I didn't necessarily want to be theirs. I wasn't sure if this would be the same for Freya.

'Sunday the 24th of April was a bright warm sunny day and we decided to go out,' I told her as I began to recount the past few weeks.

'Let's take the bikes out,' Rhys said.

'He opened the wooden shed by the front gate, we donned our helmets and set off in the direction of Califf. I pushed my bike up the incline and we whizzed down into Califf, waving to the odd passing car. The sea was azure and sparkling, the wind fresh. By the edge of the road we saw an anxious couple holding an agitated sheep in labour. Just as we were passing, the new born lamb covered in its glossy bloody placenta, was pulled from its mother's womb by the farmer.'

Freya smiled.

'Is it ok?' I asked.

'Yes, its fine, the farmer replied. 'It was in a spot of bother and needed a bit of help, but it's fine now.'

Freya gave me a questioning look.

'You see Freya,' I went on. 'Rhys being brought up in the country is used to seeing lambs being born, but I was a virgin in this respect and I stared in total awe. I am not an animal lover but I felt slightly jealous of that special connection a farmer has with his livestock and the joy and anxiety of every new birth.'

'Yes, that's special.' Freya smiled again.

'On the way back we zipped down and I was doing fine until Rhys asked, 'stop for a photograph?' I slowed down but somehow wobbled across the road and straight into a steep ditch on the opposite side of the road. I felt the handlebars in my chest and a wet muddy sensation rise in my back. At that moment a white van came past and stopped.'

'Yes?' Freya asked.

'Well. At home white van man equates with road rage, but the Shetland white van man stepped over me like a mute archangel, picking my bike off my chest and offering a helping hand to get me on my feet. Then, without a word he jumped into his van and was off.'

Freya smiled once more. I could see in her eyes that she was struggling with the subtext of my account.

'Is there something else that you want to tell me here?'

'What I am avoiding by telling you all this Freya, is.'

'Yes?' she encouraged.

'We've decided to leave Shetland when our year is up.'

'Oh, I'm so sorry to hear that.'

'Yes, and after making that very difficult decision these special Shetland things happened. It threw everything up in the air again.'

'What about the Book Club?'

'That wasn't such a great experience. Maybe I'll leave that for now.'

'So how are you feeling now?'

'Relieved I've told you. I was dreading it. I'm going to miss you.'

Gosh, how many of my clients find it as hard to say what they really want to?

I had been a member of a book club at home for several years. We were six women, who had become quite good friends and met monthly in a pub. It had become more of a food and book club and latterly more of a food club as the pub meal was the primary focus of the evening and discussion about the book relegated to second place. So I knew the format. Well, I thought I did. I should have known it would be different in Shetland.

The first meeting was held at the Lerwick Hotel and the book for discussion was 'Woman in White', by Wilkie Collins. It was a very thick book. At home we choose thin books. I hadn't managed to get even half way through the book, although I'd done some strategic reading, like the middle bit and the last few pages, so at least I'd have some sense of the story. I entered the wine coloured room, but no-one was drinking wine. There was bottled water and imperial mints such as you get at posh conferences. There were over twenty empty hard back chairs around the table. I was beginning to feel intimidated.

'You're expecting a good crowd.' I said to Alex, the guy from the Arts Council, who was organising this in association with Shetland Island Council's Library Service. My first career had been as a librarian.
This is what librarianship should be all about, reading and discussing ideas not just putting books into Dewey decimal order.

I also knew that Alex was an author as I had emailed him about his creative writing club. From what he had told me it was an established club with a focus on Shetland writing, meaning I thought, the encouragement of storytelling through dialect, something that had been discouraged for years. I was full of praise for this. It reminded me of the 'Welsh Not' and also being discouraged from using my own London slang in stories I wrote as a teenager. The difficulty for me was I couldn't wholly understand people speaking in dialect let alone write in it, so I decided not to join that club. I had hoped that the Book Club might meet my literary interests. but now I was beginning to wonder if I was up to it.

Gradually folk started to appear at the door and ease themselves into the hard back formality of the environment. Alex to be fair was welcoming and warm,

but the fact that there were so many people made me nervous. It wouldn't have been so bad if there had been a mixture of ages and sexes, but beautiful young women with probable firsts in English from great Scottish universities kept coming. There were at least fifteen. I counted one other young man besides Alex.
Book Club in Shetland is obviously not a man's bag.

    Everyone acknowledged everyone else.
I'm an outsider and an older outsider at that.

    Then the woman in black arrived.

    'Have you started?' she asked in her soothmoother tongue. I pretended I didn't understand soothmoother and ashamedly looked away. She was a very large lady, possibly over seventeen stone. She had that total black gothic look that seems edgy and wild on a seventeen year old, but sad and desperate on a fifty something. Before she'd said anything else through her black lipstick mouth, I felt drawn and yet repelled by her at the same time.

    'It's my favourite book, I just loved it.' she said
Why don't you wait your turn, woman?

    Then I remembered what frustrated me at book club at home. It was when people started telling others what they thought of the book before everyone else was seated. I hated those conversations that people had in pairs that pre-empted a proper group discussion. But then I was probably a control freak with a Dewey Decimal compulsion. I looked to Alex to take command and facilitate the discussion. But they kept coming, some with pints, beautiful young women, bringing their chairs with them from the bar, while offering their view, mostly with humour in dialect.

Nobody would be the slightest bit interested in my views and I haven't even finished the book.

'Who managed to finish the book?' asked Alex.

Half the hands went up.

Oh good, I'm not the only one

The discussions went on and I watched as an onlooker. The woman in black continued to hold the floor and for each even slightly negative view she counter pointed and raved about the book's positive qualities. A woman in her thirties or early forties burst in.

'I'm late. You'd better get used to it,' she said, looking around nodding to those she knew and started giving her view on the book. We had only been going for about twenty minutes or so, but it felt like almost everyone had spoke, except me and a couple of others and the discussion was starting to drag. It had hardly been analytical. I felt quite shy and nervous about giving an opinion as I couldn't back it up with examples from the text. That didn't stop some. A New Zealand woman said,

'I am only half way through, but I think…'

Got to admire the cock-surety.

Then Alex, who was clearly getting bored by the superficiality of the discussion turned to a broader subject,

'Anyone read any other good books lately?'

That's always one to send my mind completely blank. It's as if I've never read a book in my life. Although I've read quite a bit; titles, authors, and themes all fade away to an empty nothing. I suddenly have no memory of anything vaguely literary. Fortunately the other members had lots of suggestions and the clock ticked around long enough for Alex to bring things to a close on time.

'The book for the next meeting is a book of poetry, by a poet called Sally Reid, entitled 'Splitting.''
Poetry. I don't do poetry. And splitting. Just what I want to do. Right now.

So ended my first and last attendance at the Lerwick Book Club.

It was the Monday morning team meeting. We normally started with a 'check-in' to share how we were and if there was anything that was troubling us, professional or personal that had the potential to impact on the meeting and our work with clients in the coming week. The check-in had been my original suggestion but over the months I felt it had deteriorated into 'What did you do at the weekend?' kind of chat. On this occasion as my colleagues recounted their busy social lives, parties, gatherings with family, community arts events, dances, and fun, I noticed my insides felt strangled, a rising sense of annoyance in my chest and arrival in my throat of a full blown jealousy attack. I had never viewed myself as the jealous sort. I had often thought of myself, modestly, as a generous hearted person, who would be genuinely pleased to hear others' good news. Seemed like I'd changed. It wasn't as if Rhys and I weren't having a good time, our weekends were full of exploration: the islands, walking, watching wild life, searching out historical places of interest. God, imagine how I'd have been without him?

It wasn't as if we had made no friends. We were sometimes invited over to these colleagues homes' and we made an effort to return hospitality. What these Monday morning meetings highlighted was the difference in our circumstances. All my colleagues had another life, involving other friends and family. Individually, they had shown kindness outside of work that was way above what was reasonable to expect of colleagues. However, that whingeing, whining, ghastly, grabbing inner child, left on her own in hospital aged 18months and a mother who died on her when she was 20 years old kept shouting, 'What about me? What about me?' I had, what in the counselling trade was called, an 'entitlement schema,' an unreasonable expectation that I should have more attention and I needed to manage it.

When it got to my turn I shared my concerns about the children and recounted that Liam was into extreme sports.

'I do extreme sports,' said Emily.

Are you going to top me again, Emily?

I ignored her. I felt some resentment bubbling.

'Yes, I did extreme ironing at the weekend.'

Everyone laughed.

Ok, very funny. Now, back to me please. Talk about me.

'No, really I did. We were attempting to break the record and get into the Guinness Book of Records.'

'Oh yes?'

'So we took the ironing board and a pile of ironing onto a dingy and rowed out to the Viking Ship anchored in the bay at Baltasound. We took lots of photos of us doing extreme ironing, left a few bits of evidence, like sexy underwear tied to the mast and rowed back in the dingy.'

Jealousy attack imminent! Why didn't you ask me? I'd loved to have done that.

Emily had worked as a producer for BBC Plymouth years ago, and what I really enjoyed about her was her sense of the bizarre. For example, Bobby's Bus Shelter, done out like someone's front room, with ornaments, armchair, net curtains, TV, computer, radio, toaster, none of which was connected to the mains. It was a piece of performance art, had become a tourist attraction on the most northerly of the British Isles and I loved it. Extreme ironing was another example of people in rural areas making their own fun. It took me back to twenty years ago, when Rhys and I ran a community arts group in our village.

Come on, give her credit, you jealous cow.

'That's hilarious, Emily. Wish I'd been there to see it,'

'Emily has a tremendous capacity to embrace the bizarre,' said Calum laughing. 'Shall we move on?'

Weekly Routine

May 2005

On May 4 we drove the twenty five mile trip down to Sumburgh airport to pick up Frida. Her journey had been uneventful; one flight cancelled, delays and her suitcase lost in transit. Not bad from Gatwick.

Frida and I had been colleagues at the Royal College of Nursing, where we counselled nurse members. I had liked her from the very first day I met her. It was my first team meeting in Croydon, where the UK team of seven counsellors met on a quarterly basis and I knew no-one except the manager. She greeted everyone warmly with a large bear hug. She must have seen that I was feeling a bit left out. Although we'd never met before and a handshake might have been the most touchy-feely one would have expected at a first meet, she embraced me fully into her matronly bosom.

Frida was born and brought up in the States but had lived in the UK for over twenty five years. She had been a nursing sister working with the terminally ill before having a change of focus and a new career as a psychotherapist and counsellor. More recently her interest in the spiritual and the world of the unconscious had widened. Frida has a natural gift for healing and to spend time with her always feels therapeutic.

When I knew I was coming to Shetland she did an imaginary journey for me. Journeying has been part of many cultures, particularly the North American Indians, who might go out into the wilderness, possibly imbibing some herbs that would put them into a trance like state and help communication with the other world. The Delphi Oracle is another example. Frida didn't imbibe herbs or go into a trance like state. It seemed more like having a dream, but being awake. The important thing seemed to be asking the right kind of question. Frida asked the universe the question,

'What wisdom does Jan need on the next phase of her life's journey?'

This is the account of Frida's visualization/journey as she related it to me:

'I met a white horse in a field, we rode to a cave and went in. At the end was a chamber, where we met Hercules, a ferryman. It was a cell-like cave with an old table with a single drawer and a box on it. I asked the question, and Hercules said, pointing up to a square window with bars on it in the ceiling,

'Tell her to look up to things of the spirit. She is to take what is in the drawer.'

Frida opened it to find a silver cutlery set, like the family silver.

'Next we looked in the box. It was dark brown, made of wood, shaped like a treasure chest with gold studs on the top and gold fasteners like those you might find on a toolbox or trunk. Inside was a jumble of old jewellery. I saw a string of pearls, a copper bracelet and some plastic costume jewellery. He said,

'Tell her to sort through this; keep what is of value, repair what is broken, and discard the junk.'

Then I saw a beautiful silver ring on a tray at the top. It was new and had a red stone, jasper, at one end and a green one, moss agate, at the other.

'Tell her to wear this - it will help her discern what is true.'

Then Frida turned to the right and saw an old desk in an alcove. It had pigeonholes and files of papers stacked all around it. The space on its surface was clear.

'These are her life's experiences. Tell her to sort them out, and then she may write them down.' Frida noticed there was no chair to sit and write.

'She will be given one when the time comes.'
Frida asked, 'And when she has done this?' I had a sense of a room beyond the door of the cave.

'She will have much to offer and somewhere to go.'

Frida said, 'She is concerned about dying.'

He said, 'All will be well.'

When Frida recounted her visualization to me a couple of months before coming to Shetland I was fascinated by its imagery and eager to learn what it might mean once I was established.

A few days after we first arrived in Shetland we were browsing aimlessly across Strand Loch from our sitting room armchairs, when I saw an elderly white horse grazing at the water's edge.

'Look, Frida's with us,' I exclaimed to Rhys.

Luckily, Rhys is very receptive to imagery and the unconscious and didn't respond by calling me bonkers; many would. Over the year the old white horse came down to greet us regularly in all weathers and we became very fond of her.

Frida is also great fun so I was really looking forward to the few days we would spend together.

'God, it's amazing,' she said, when she saw the view from the lounge window.

'Bleak', is what some have called it,' I replied.

'Then they have no soul,' she said as she took her specs off, rubbed her eyes and breathed in our new world.

'Wait until you see Papil.' I replied.

The North Atlantic surf was at its best for tourists although probably not for sailors on the day we took Frida to Papil; a white Sargasso sea. We were well wrapped up in several layers. Rhys had lent Frida his trusty balaclava that seemed to have become standard use for all our visitors. Her specs misted up as the wind buffed and grazed our exposed bits. Armed with my ski pole walking aid and heavy boots, Frida looked like she was about to set out on an Antarctic expedition. She followed me across the beach against the wind. When I glanced back I saw her looking down anxiously at her small feet wobbling with the stick over the stones on the bank.

'You're not happy, are you? What's wrong?' I said trying to stifle a grin.

'The idea of being out in the elements often contrasts with the reality. It annoys me that I'm annoyed by it.'

'Here, take my hand,' I said pulling her up. 'Remember camping?'

'Only too well.'

We both threw our heads back and laughed loudly.

Frida in her 53 years had never been camping. She had been going on to me for ages how much she wanted to go, be close to the earth, feel the connection with the land etc., but every time I suggested she join Rhys and I in Pembrokeshire she found a reason to shy off. But the previous year she committed herself to a night under nylon. The weather was good, but the temperature dropped as she bedded down. All seemed to go well, until the middle of the night, when she awoke to a hissing noise; the airbed had a puncture and the ground was compacted and hard. She also needed a pee. The loo was some way off so she used a trick she had been told about by a friend, who had probably never been camping either, to use a hot water bottle. She then needed a shower but because we were asleep, and she didn't want to wake us, she headed for the facilities, not knowing until too late that to have a hot shower you needed a token. We awoke sometime later to find one wet cold grumpy Frida on the step of our caravan eager to warm up and have breakfast.

'These things are often fun in retrospect,' I told her encouragingly.

We walked up onto the spit of land above Papil's turquoise beach and went off in our own wandering directions. After a while I looked around.

'Where's Frida?' I asked Rhys.

Grinning, he pointed down to what looked like a large green creature laying horizontal on the slope.

'Feel the energy of this place,' Frida shouted.

I ran down the slope and plonked myself down beside her.

'Didn't your mother tell you never to lie on wet patches?' I asked.

'My mother told me a whole load of things I don't remember. Can you feel the connection?'

I looked up at the sky, white bunny clouds bouncing across my vision, the wind rubbing my nose, the dampish earth throbbing beneath my back.

'Yes, I can. This gives a whole different perspective. Did I tell you this is a holy place? It's the site of a monastery. Papil means hermit in Old Norse.'

'Then I'm not imagining it,' Frida murmured.

Rhys looked on smiling at the two large horizontal mounds, one green one red.

'Is anyone hungry?' he asked.

'You are!' I laughed.

'Come on, join us,' Frida said from the ground, but Rhys's stomach was making noises that were hard to ignore.

'It looks like rain too. We're invited to Maggie and Bob's tonight and you can always guarantee a good feed. Time to go.'

By the time we had reached the car there was a strong horizontal rain.

'How extraordinary,' said Frida. 'My left side is completely sodden from balaclava to boot, but my right side is absolutely dry.'

When Maggie and Bob knew we had a friend coming from down south they suggested we bring her over to dinner. They were always interested in meeting new people and were kind and generous in their hospitality.

'Is that a peat fire?' asked Frida, as she picked up a hunk of earth from the basket by the fire, putting it close to her nose, crumbling the sod in her hand and sniffing in the smell of centuries.

'Wow, that's wonderful,' she said, drawing herself nearer to the Rowlands's hearth.

'Do you collect this yourselves?' she asked.

'We used to,' said Maggie. We have crofter's rights to cutting peat from an area a little way away. It is a long process. All the family and neighbours were involved. George Mackay, the Orcadian poet described the process as 'tearing dark squares, thick pages from the book of fire.'

'Tell me more,' said Frida.

'The work took up most of the summer. The banks were sliced and cut in April or May as the weather permitted. It was very important that there was no possibility of frost as that would make it useless for burning. The peat was raised and turned and left to dry out. You can still see mounds or triangles of peat bricks drying by the side of the road now. When the peat was dry enough the children might bring it home in a wheelbarrow, on horseback in a peat creel, or the women would carry it on their backs in a specially made basket, called a kishie. It was hard work but now we buy the peat from a local supplier.'

'Isn't it quite controversial to use peat now? Although the svagnum moss, from which peat is formed holds carbon, peat omits it and some believe that as a consequence it contributes to greenhouse warming,' I said.

'Poppycock,' responded Maggie in her usual matter of fact way. 'It causes less damage in the quantities it is used here in Shetland than say coal would. It's never been commercially exploited here and now not many folk use it as their main source of energy.'

Maggie loved talking about her family's history and Shetland customs. The family's bookshelves were full of history, geology, birds, wildlife, and she and Bob were a fount of local knowledge.

'What an interesting evening and such nice people,' said Frida on the way home.

'Yes, we've been very lucky to have met them. They've enriched our stay here.'

Later on in her stay I asked Frida to do another journey for me. The question I needed an answer to was, 'What wisdom do I need to take from Shetland into the next phase of my life?'

In her imagination, Frida started from Papil beach. This is what she recounted to me;

'The white horse along with the ferryman met me. We got into his boat and he rowed to a cave in the rocks. As we were rowing across I asked the ferryman, *'What wisdom does Jan need to take into her next phase of life?'*

He was an elderly seaman in a black sou'wester and answered,

'The wisdom of the wind, the wisdom of the sea and the wisdom of the hills.'

'When we arrived at the cave the ferryman showed us into a room. It was like the cave room in the previous journey, but the walls were lined with bookshelves tidily full of books, model ships and pictures. There was a leaded window at the top facing the doors. There was a table with a jewellery box on it. I noticed a candle burning on the desk; a white dinner candle in a brass holder.'

'Tell her, to make sure this doesn't go out,' the ferryman said.

Then he opened the jewellery box and held several strands of beads up.

'She has sorted these out; tell her to start wearing them.'

Then I asked the ferryman, 'What do the books on the shelves mean?'

'These are the books she needs to write,' he said.

Then he spun around and became a youngish woman dressed in 18-19th century wedding gear, with a tiara of flowers in her hair, looking wistfully out of the window, waiting for her beloved to come back from the sea.

'What does it mean?' Frida asked and had the sense that there is something I must wait for. 'Then the bride became the ferryman once more, and he drew a box out from under the table. It contained an old fashioned sewing machine.'

'These are the things she needs to mend,' he said.

'What else, what else?' I asked Frida.

'That's it, nothing else. The journey ended there,' Frida said. 'Now, what about a cup of tea, I'm parched.'

The following evening Frida also did a version of the Tarot with me, called 'The Green Man,' which had cards, each with a tree or a plant that has a specific value and meaning. The cards I chose were holly and rowen representing connection, protection, and communication.

As we saw her off onto her plane back to the south of England I was left with a lot to think about. As soon as I got back to the office I decided to check out on the internet what the significance of jasper and moss-agate might be. For jasper I read,

'Jasper is known as the supreme nurturer. It sustains and supports during time of stress and brings tranquillity and wholeness. Used in healing it signifies all aspects of your life. Jasper reminds people to help each other.'

And,

'Moss Agate is a stabilising stone connected with nature. It is said to refresh the soul and enables you to see the beauty in all you behold. It is helpful in reducing sensitivity to weather and environmental pollutants... it promotes self-expression and communication.'

A few days later the sea was calm but there was a cold wind as I made my early morning way through the Lerwick lanes to Freya's studio for an art therapy session a few days after Frida's departure. I told her about the 'journeys' I had done with Frida and we chewed over what it could all possibly mean.

I also told Freya about an experience I had on a psychotherapy weekend course a couple of years before, when during a visualization exercise I had a powerful image confront me; it was a claymore as I imagined used by Braveheart, but it also looked like the kind of stick that represented healing in ancient times; a staff with a jewel in its handle and a green snake curling up its blade. During the exercise the snake wound itself around my body up to my neck, where it started to strangle me, then the claymore of its own accord began violently to take swipes at me and chopped me into pieces. I was completely annihilated.

The exercise left me very shaken. The tutor suggested that this imagery could relate to early childhood trauma and that it might be helpful to explore it with a psychotherapist. I had not done so at the time. I just wanted to put it away. It was too disturbing. She said and I believed that I may be particularly susceptible to visual imagery, which although on this occasion was disturbing could be used in a positive way.

To gain more insight into my creative unconscious world was the reason I had chosen to work with an art therapist over a traditional counsellor or psychotherapist. My main model of counselling clients was integrative; integrating person centred, solution focused and cognitive behavioural therapies, very useful for working in the NHS, with clients suffering from anxiety and depression but limited in its understanding of the unconscious. I felt very comfortable to discuss imagery with Freya. I knew she would not force her own interpretation on to it but would help me find my own meaning from it.

I had thought a lot about the image over the past couple of years and discussed it with Frida, who thought that it might be an image of transformation. I liked that idea and wondered what it might mean for me. Now in Shetland, when I thought about the image, the claymore had changed more into a cross. I wondered if I was going to become a born again

Christian. I had always been closed to organised religion, having spent the first sixteen years of my life brought up as a Catholic and a very reluctant and bolshie teenage one at that. At this stage in my life I felt more open to the world of the spiritual but couldn't quite see myself having a 'Saul on the road to Damascus' kind of conversion. Shetland in Old Norse, Hjaltland, meant sword, as the shape of the isles form a claymore type sword. Perhaps this experience was predicting that I would come to Shetland and she would offer me transformation. Indeed, in Shetland, more than anywhere else I had been I did feel a connection to the island elements, raw and wild and I knew at some level it was this sense of the spiritual that would be with me when I took the final ferry homeward bound.

On arriving at work after my art therapy session, I noticed that I had lost the serpent shaped connector that held my amethyst necklace in place. Then a few days later, browsing in the Shetland Times Bookshop, I flicked through a book on the Picts, the early ancestors of the Scots, and found that a Pictish serpent was a symbol of wisdom and healing. The problem in believing in the inter-connectedness of the universe is that you look for a connection in everything. Sometimes it's very useful in order to gain insight and understanding but at other times it's confusing. It could send you mad.

If I'm not careful I'll start believing in conspiracy theories next.

A couple of days later a small package arrived for me from Frida. It contained a piece of jasper and moss agate.

'This has been the worst year of my life,' Rachel told me on the telephone one light evening towards the end of May. She had had a very difficult day on teaching practice. The journey to and from the school was a thirty mile round trip by an unreliable Ford Fiesta. The school was another tough valleys school and her mentor was inexperienced. She had been given a hotchpotch of classes and levels to teach, and far more than the recommended number. It seemed like there was some kind of power struggle going on between the school and the university and she was caught in the middle. Staff gathered in their cliques in the staff room at breaks and she felt isolated and excluded. So, she took to working alone through her breaks, which compounded her isolation.

At home the lodger, 'Big Jen', as Rachel had nicknamed her, because of her size and her propensity to eat take-aways and Christmas size tins of chocolates, was a total disaster. Jen stayed in her room, which emitted smells of staleness and old food, didn't socialize and never helped with chores. It sounded as if Jen was depressed.

Our house was rather large for one busy person to manage and Rachel was really struggling with keeping the house clean, doing her academic assignments, preparing lessons and marking. She rarely got to bed before midnight and was up early to leave the house by 7.30am. She was exhausted, demoralized and lonely. She had no social life or time to spend with her friends. She seemed on the verge of giving up.

I felt very guilty and powerless. Apart from encouraging telephone calls and throwing in ideas, despite never having taught children in my life, there was not much I or Rhys could do to help. We felt anxious for her. Again, too far away and too expensive to fly home for a weekend visit. Friends had said that our going away would be an opportunity for Rachel to grow and become independent, but hearing her nightly misery triggered off all the old feelings I had about not being a good mother. She never once asked me to come home, but it reinforced my view that home for me was being somewhere geographically available to support our children, when they most needed it. It also reinforced my belief that we were making the right decision to return home after a year living and working in Shetland.

This was a difficult one to discuss with Shetlanders, who knew that their children would probably have to leave the islands if they wanted to go into higher education or find work. They *had* to emotionally adjust to separation and loss. Children on the outer islands moved to Lerwick as secondary school boarders at the age of 15, some younger. When they left home at 17, the likelihood was that apart from an annual holiday and maybe Christmas, many families would see very little of each other; that is until the young folk wanted to start families of their own and Shetland might draw them back home again.

'Rachel will probably leave the country to work once you return or at least leave home to share with friends. You've said so yourself. Why plan your lives around your children at this stage?' asked Maggie, when I called her to tell her how things were with our daughter and our plans to leave after a year. I knew Maggie was only voicing what many Shetlanders were probably thinking about us.
I know I am a total woos.
   'Well, I wouldn't mind that. It will probably happen but it would be her decision. I now know that in the longer term being so far away from my family won't work for me.'
Well, I think I know.

'Are you coming to Philosophy Club on Friday?' Roger asked me as I popped into the kitchen to fill the kettle for the counselling team's Monday meeting. While working as a domestic, washing up the endless cups, saucers, plates, Roger, in his seventies, spiked up his working day by listening to Radio 4 or whistling classical tunes. After his daily shift he would go swimming at the local leisure centre and then come back to eat his lunch in the staff canteen at Montfield. He was always ravenous despite having a small wiry frame and the canteen ladies piled his plate with a volcano of vegetables topped with a small tin of fish that I think he brought in from home. He usually had a large tome of something intellectual to accompany his meal.

'Err,'

How do I get out of this one?

'It's at Deirdre's on Friday 7.30pm.' His cyan blue eyes held my gaze waiting for a reply.

'Yes, we would love to,' I lied. 'See you later.'

'Oh, and the subject of the meeting is quantum mechanics.'

Right.

'What's quantum mechanics?" Rhys asked, as I told him about Friday.

'I haven't got a clue.'

It's a real disadvantage being in a relationship where your opposite number is as poorly informed as you are about science. It means you have to ask someone else.

'Well, it's complicated. How long have you got?' Calum asked, when I caught him later that week coming out of Montfield en route to Levenwick. I had decided on asking Calum as he had a B.Sc. and he was one of the few people I knew who spanned three disciplines; counselling, divinity and science. Also, he knew how scientifically illiterate I was so there was no point in bluffing.

'Two days.'

'Oh dear. I'll send you some references.' He scanned my anxious face.

'Don't worry,' he grinned. 'You'll be fine. See it as an opportunity for learning.'

I will worry and No, I won't be fine, thank you Calum.

That Friday was the first bright evening in May to remind us summer was on its way. We followed the coastal road towards Sumburgh. The sea was azure like the colour of the Mediterranean and the countryside was bathed in sharp light throwing long shadows across the hills. We had talked about crying off, but we liked the people in the group and thought it would seem rude to turn down the invitation when we had no other plans. So we geared ourselves up for ignorance and humiliation.

We hadn't met Deirdre before as she'd been in hospital at the last meeting at Roger's home. She had a beautifully renovated croft overlooking fields and the sea near Sandwick, where she lived with her husband and children. An attractive middle-aged woman with dark wavy hair, Deirdre welcomed us warmly into her home and it was clear that she, Jack and Roger had been friends for a long time. A music teacher at the local comprehensive school, Deirdre was also one of the original founders of the Club.

We sat down and she started to talk on the theme of quantum mechanics. Jack, an ex-meteorological man turned crofter and Roger, an ex-teacher, musician and domestic, listened attentively and made intelligent comments about scientists I had never heard of. Deirdre kept referring to the second law of thermodynamics. Seeing Rhys and I frowning she asked,

   'Do you know what that is?'
No, and I won't understand when you explain it to me either.
   After several attempts to explain how information is physical and other concepts, I noticed that Rhys was tugging the loose skin under his chin, a sure sign of anxiety. I smiled encouragingly.
We're stupid. GET US OUT OF HERE!
   The group were very polite but it was evident that we were clueless and could contribute nothing, not even an interesting question or comment to the discussion or the evening. We had been well and truly rumbled. However, the whole evening was not a total disaster. After the hour long lecture and discussion, in Shetland fashion we all sat down to a splendid meal. This gave us the opportunity to ask questions to Deirdre about croft renovation, a subject I also knew nothing about but with a full mouth of food it was somewhat easier not to frown through the whole lengthy response.

   'You are all invited to a PURE open day on Sunday 23rd May,' announced Emily at the next counselling team meeting.
   'What's PURE?' Tracy asked.

'Well, certainly not you, darling,' I quipped. She gave me a wink and that Bolton Wanderers grin.

'Promoting Unst Renewable Energy. There will be the best of the island's cuisine; fresh salmon, handmade chocolates, local beer, good bands and a chance to drive the hydrogen generated prototype car.'

'Sounds good, Emily. I'll talk to Rhys. Will you go, Tracy?' She gave me that look of 'and miss me footie?' Instead she said,

'I'll let you know later on in the week.'

'We're expecting a crowd, so if you're coming don't forget to book the ferries,' Emily added.

'Now children, social life all sorted, what about some work?' Calum asked.

'I wish I'd listened to Emily about booking the ferries,' I said meekly to Rhys as we sat in a long line of cars at Toft. It didn't look likely that we would get on the incoming ferry.

'When's the next one?' Rhys asked.

'I'll go and look.' I wandered along the quay.

Oh dear, I hadn't reckoned on a Sunday service.

'The next one is in an hour and a half to Ulsta in Yell and then we've got to get the smaller ferry from Gutcher,' I said to Rhys as I got back in the car. 'I guess it's too late to pre-book that one.'

The cars filed off and onto the ferry and the crew member waved down the car three vehicles ahead of us. No more spaces.

'Damn, we'll miss the buffet.' I said.

I'm having a sense of déjà vu. Remember Christmas?

Other folk were making up their mind by pulling their cars out of the queue behind us. It was already gone 12 noon. It would hardly be worth going.

'What do you think?' I asked Rhys.

'Well, it's not dark until 10pm so we could go for a walk on Hermaness and see the puffins and still get to see something of the PURE project,' said Rhys generously.

If it had been him that hadn't booked the ferry and as a result we'd missed out, I would have been at least a tad acerbic. How lucky I'd married an adult.

I bet you're thinking about the missed buffet and free beer.

'Look, what's that in the middle distance?' Rhys muttered.

'Here, use the binoculars.'

He took the binoculars and scanned the horizon.

'It's a ferry. But how?'

The crew had given up their lunch break so that wasters like us, who hadn't booked the ferry could get to Unst for the open day. Instead of waiting an hour and a half, the wait was just twenty minutes.

'I can't imagine that happening anywhere elsewhere but Shetland, can you?' I said.

'No, indeed. Coming up top for a coffee?'

Unst is the most northerly populated island in the British Isles, in 2005 there were around 800 people and over 100,000 breeding sea birds co-habiting. According to the people's website the island was 'unique in terms of its scenic beauty and mystical charm.' On the first occasion I visited I would have translated mystical charm as desolate, but Unst had grown on me over the months, particularly since I had started seeing clients from there fortnightly. This would be the first time I had visited the national nature reserve. The only problem I could foresee were the bonxies.

The interior of Hermaness was blanket bog, an internationally rare habitat, 'where the visitor', again quoting the website, 'runs the gauntlet of the nesting great skua' or as they are known locally 'the bonxie"
I love watching birds now, but two issues have affected my enjoyment of them. Firstly, as a very small child my father would let our pet budgie out of its cage to fly around the kitchen for the sport of watching my mother, who would become hysterical, scream and run out.

'Is it back yet?' heard from behind the kitchen door, was one my earliest verbal memories. I learnt from my mother that birds were dangerous. I developed pteraphobia, a fear of wings, or in my case birds in flight landing on me. In London as a teenager I would cross the road if a pigeon was in my path. On the Underground pigeons occasionally got trapped in railway carriages between stations. On one occasion I grabbed an Evening Standard out of the hand of a fellow traveller, covered my head with it, and threw myself to the floor commando style. No-one round me showed the slightest concern or surprise; Tube travellers are used to totally ignoring nutters.

The second event was the Alfred Hitchcock film, 'The Birds', with its nightmare images of children and adults being pursued by huge sea-birds and pecked to death.

'Why did I say I'd do this?' I asked Rhys, as I put on my cycle helmet and he tied a couple of bright scarves to the Norwegian poles that helped steady me on unsteady walks.

Is this my punishment for a missed buffet?

'Hold one of these high above your head and if one comes near wave it and then the bonxie won't attack you. They are just protecting their young.'

'Am I being paranoid or did those people look at me in a funny way?' I asked my bird loving husband, as I held my ski pole above my head like a Unicorn's spiralled horn.

'Perhaps, because we haven't reached the nesting ground. It's some way yet.'

'Why do we have to go through the nesting ground?'

'To reach the cliffs and the puffins. As long as we're quiet and respectful of their space we should be fine.'

Great skuas spend most of the year on the ocean, only coming to land to breed between April and September. Until 80 years ago they were found only on two of the Shetland Islands, Unst and Foula but now they breed in smaller numbers elsewhere and in the Outer Hebrides, the Orkneys and in Caithness and Sutherland. Slow and heavy in normal flight, the great skua turns into a skilful flyer when it hunts, twisting from side to side as it chases a gull as big as itself. They feed mainly on fish stolen by forcing other birds to disgorge. Both parents prepare the nest, incubate the two olive green eggs with their dark brown blotches and tend the nestlings, until after 40-50 days the baby bonxies finally fly away. Our bird book told us that, 'parent great skuas have been seen to cling to the head of an intruding sheep and batter it with their wings until the bruised animal is driven away.'

'What's that over there?'
'Probably a gull.'
Right. You don't lie dear husband, but are you just telling me what I want and need to hear?

'Fight or Flight,' is the state of anxiety that I had lectured my clients on hundreds of times. It's a reaction that emanates from when human beings lived in caves and were faced with real danger like the possibility of being attacked by a lion, leopard or something life threatening. You stayed to fight, you played dead or you ran away. Anyone who has been in a life threatening situation where they think they might die, such as a train crash or a bank robbery, or someone with an irrational fear of something, like public speaking or tomatoes, will understand that awful sense of fear and panic that I felt as I realized that there wasn't one but many large brown bonxies sitting on nests well camouflaged in the sepia tinted peat and heather bog.

'Just keep walking,' Rhys said encouragingly.

'Why don't they just have a visitors hide, like the one on Fetlar. Then you could watch them safely from afar.'

'Then you wouldn't get to see the puffins on the cliffs opposite Muckle Flugga.'

Do I care about seeing the puffins? At this moment, I don't think so.

'Maybe if I whistle a happy tune like Julie Andrews in the Sound of Music? Nah, they'd probably mistake it for an unhappy tune and take it as a sign to attack,' I mused.

Just as the words had left my mouth I saw from the corner of my eye that we were uncomfortably close to a nest and the bird on it was not happy. The hawk like bird raised itself slowly up from the nest; I saw a flash of a white-patch, it flew high and then lower, sweeping down to have a good look and then - whoosh, that scene from Alfred Hitchcock replayed many times before in my imagination - now seemed to be acted out for real.

Stay calm! Stay calm!

'They attack with their feet. Janet, wave the stick!' Rhys shouted. I felt nauseous and I felt my heart danced the jive to the rhythm of a deafening bass drum. I looked at Rhys, who was just walking forward calmly waving a ski pole high above his head, the pink scarf seeming to frighten the bird away.

'Rhys, WAIT FOR ME!' I shouted, breaking into a stumble.

'Come on we're nearly at the cliffs and you can enjoy the antics of the puffins.'

I can't wait. Breathe! Wave your stick! Breathe! Stay calm!

As we got nearer we saw a couple sitting very still on the very edge of the turf-covered sea cliffs. The young man seemed to be pointing his mobile at something obscured from our view.

'Don't go too near the edge Rhys,' I called in a maternal tone that probably made his insides curl. After saving him from the bonxies I didn't want to lose him in a cliff fall to the puffins. I had spent most of my married life tightening my fists and gasping, while watching my husband jump across rocks on the side of precipices, climb tall trees, enter disused lead mines, or get to work on time by the skin of his teeth. I was a total cowardy custard. I didn't take physical risks like that. My co-ordination and ankles were weak after years of wearing unsuitable footwear. I'd gone over too many London curbs wearing platform shoes in the '70s. I also left for work in good time. Liam our son had the same approach to life as his father, but they now call life on the edge an extreme sport. Rachel seemed to be going in the same direction.

'Come over here, you'll get a better view,' he said.

No, I don't think so, thank you.

'Please Rhys, you're making me nervous.'

As I edged my bottom nearer to see the puffins I saw the sign, 'DANGER! SLIDING WEATHERPROOF TROUSERS!' I reversed back quickly.

Puffins in Shetland are known as 'tammie norries.' These small funny looking birds are instantly recognizable by their huge bill, like a bright triangular flag of red, blue and yellow as they come in from the Atlantic to breed in summer months. Both sexes dig burrows in turf or under boulders with their bills, or occupy old shearwater or rabbit burrows. Puffins thrust their bills at neighbours as a threat and toss their heads hiding their bills if they want to make peace. In recent years numbers of tammy norries in Shetland had declined dramatically. It is thought that this is due to the decrease in their main food supply - sand eels - whose breeding grounds had been disturbed over the years by deep-sea dredging.

I sat still at a safe distance, while Rhys got nearer. I watched as he photographed the birds flying in and out of their burrows, shovelling away the loose earth with their webbed feet, squeaking puffin talk, coming and going with mouthfuls of grass and feathers to line their nests. They didn't seem too bothered by us and as long as I was at a distance I didn't feel too anxious. I just kept a vigilant eye out for any marauding bonxies.

We continued along the cliff and saw many other sea-birds below us, including gannets, which have their own colony on Muckle Flugga, a rocky outlet in the far north of Unst. The lighthouse was built in 1858 during the Crimean war by David and Thomas Stevenson. It was said that their nephew, Robert Louis wrote 'Treasure Island' following a visit to Unst. We looked down. The sea crashed against the white rock, bleached by years of defecating birds.

'A lonely and isolated place to be a lighthouse keeper,' I said, but Rhys' binoculars were focused on the gannets.

'My mother always called me a gannet, partly because it rhymed with Janet but mainly because as a growing teenager, I dived into the fridge like one.' But Rhys wasn't really listening. He'd probably heard it before.

'There's a signpost to the right, back to the visitor centre. Shall we go?' I asked after a while.

I looked across the bog with its oily streams running in the early evening light, the dark pungent earth fragmented in humps and bumps and tried not to think of bonxies. We tried to walk at a pace across the bog but it was like walking up and down large stairs, springy but uneven and great for trapping weak ankles.

When we had got three quarters of the way across I realized that I hadn't noticed any nesting bonxies close by. I turned to Rhys,

'Don't tell me, if we'd taken the Muckle Flugga path I wouldn't have..,' but it was no use, his mind was set on his stomach.

'You've missed the speeches and the buffet but you might be lucky with the beer,' Emily said, as we ambled into the marquee, dirty, thirsty and hungry to the evening of the PURE open day.

A smiling gentleman wearing a T shirt with 'Valhalla Brewery' on his chest, pulled a pint of local brew and then another.

'You're lucky. I didn't think we'd get another two,' he said thrusting plastic glasses into our hands.

We drank the Viking brew thankfully and then strolled outside to see what was happening. There weren't many people about, but I kept my head down just in case I saw any of my clients. As a counsellor there was a kind of unwritten rule; unless a client acknowledges you, you don't acknowledge them. For many it was still a stigma to see a counsellor and clients often didn't want anyone including or sometimes especially their close relatives to know they had been seeing you. How else would they know this foreigner in a small community?

'Hi, Janet and Rhys.' I looked up and saw Donald, Emily's husband coming towards us. 'Have you had a ride in the hydrogen generated car? Come on and give it a spin.'

In the parking area a shiny lime box resembling a Mini car was going around in circles driven by a ten year old. While we waited for her to finish Rhys and I grilled Donald on the project.

'The PURE Project is an off-grid stand-alone system, which allows wind generated electricity to convert water into hydrogen. The hydrogen is then bottled and kept for converting back into electricity- as and when required-producing water as the only waste product from the entire process. The cycle can then be repeated. The car runs on a battery that has hydrogen fuel cells. The system was the idea of Ross, a local Shetland engineering graduate.' Donald waved down the little girl, and asked her politely if she would mind if someone else had a go.

'Go on get in, try it.' Rhys got in. 'There are no gears, it's automatic and can reach a speed of about 35miles an hour. It's obviously a prototype and at the moment you can't go far because the battery needs regular re-charging.'

'Fine, for visiting other islanders or the local shop,' I said, repeating the process in my mind.
Concentrate. This is science but you can understand it if you focus. Try.

'At the moment, but this is the fuel of the future. It burns no fossil fuels and there are no carbon emissions.'

Rhys got out and I tentatively got in. I drove cautiously at about five miles an hour.

'It's so quiet. It's like being on a fairground ride.'

'Not the dodgems at that speed,' laughed Donald.

'Donald is a very modest person, isn't he?" I said to Rhys, as we bid farewell and drove our grubby green Peugeot 306 to the ferry. 'You know what he didn't say is that he is at the forefront of economic regeneration in Unst.'

'Yes, I read somewhere that the PURE project is the first community owned hydrogen production plant in the world. The wind turbine also generates electricity for the community, the hall and the school, I think.'

'I am sure that's due largely to his skill as an entrepreneur and a facilitator.'

'Unst will need something when the RAF eventually pulls out,' Rhys replied.

It was still light as we got on the 10pm ferry at Belmont. As we drove across Yell to get to the second ferry we looked across Blue Mull Sound at the twinkling lights of the Sullom Voe oil terminal, one of the biggest in Europe.

'I hope they give PURE a chance,' murmured Rhys.

'Don't worry, Donald and his band, 'The Bonxies' will give them a good run for their money.'

Bobby's Bus Shelter

Bobby's Bus Shelter

Peat

June 2005

'Jesus Saves,' read the hand painted cloth sign at the back of the 52 seater coach parked by Tingwall public hall.

'He's been there for a few days, I said to Rhys as I peered sideways out of the living room window. 'I thought I saw the coach in Whalsay last week. He must live on the coach.'

'Well, it looks like he's fishing for his supper,' replied Rhys. We looked out at the pearly peach loch reflecting a soft sunset. It was 10pm and there would still be at least another hour of light.

'The fish are jumping for him, look!' I exclaimed. I always thought 'fish jumping' was just a line in a Rogers and Hammerstein movie.

'They aren't jumping for him, they're jumping for insects,' Rhys said.

'They aren't just jumping, they're <u>leaping</u> out of the water. There are hundreds across the loch.'

'Why can't they do that for me?' Rhys whined.

Poor him, he'd had several attempts at fishing with the starter pack he bought at the Rod and Line shop. His barber had even taken him out one dull evening to give him a few tips, but they both came back without anything for our tea. Something about there being a lot of gnats and it being a bad year for fishing. *Yeh, right.*

We watched the wadered fisherman move towards the centre of the loch casting his line again and again.

'Perhaps he's fishing for the five thousand,' I mused.

'Hey, you haven't even opened your starter pack yet,' Rhys teased.

'No, that's because my idea of fishing is whiling away a warm sunny afternoon, semi comatose, a book on my lap, with the line tied to my toe for minimum discomfort and effort.'

'Brother Clifford's a cracking bloke," said Bob, about our religious fishing neighbour when we next met up. 'He comes to Shetland every year, travels across Britain and Ireland and lives in the coach. He lives by fishing and food people give him. He has a little dog for company. He welcomes anyone who wants to pop in for a chat. You should drop by.'

But the next day the coach was gone, Brother Clifford had moved on.

'The Field Studies Group has an interesting programme of events,' said Rhys one June evening, as we sat post-dinner slump watching the TV news.

'Oh yes, what's on?'

'That woman, Jill Blackadder is leading a walk on Nesting this weekend.'

The name conjured images of Rowan Atkinson and Stephen Fry in the trenches in WW1, but the Essex

primary school teacher had lived in Shetland for over twenty years and wrote a weekly wild life article in the Shetland Times. She had endeared herself to me in a recent article about a hedgehog that she took on a trip home. It escaped and she found herself in the long grass of her Essex garden at midnight calling its name - and the hedgehog came back.
Certainly breaks the usual stereotype of Essex girls.

We were picked up in a minibus en route the following Sunday afternoon. Jill Blackadder got out and introduced herself; a small blue-eyed red head, one arm hung loosely by her side and she limped. I wondered if she had had a stroke.

Nesting is a low-lying area in the east mainland. There are many pre-historic houses, cairns, burnt mounds, and at this time of the year it had an abundance of wild flowers. Laxo in the north of Nesting is where I would take the ferry to Whalsay. The Field Studies group had been given permission by the local landowner to walk its members around some fields in the south, which had rare orchids and other species.

In the minibus were a few Shetlanders, a soothmoother couple, who had just moved to Shetland and were doing up an old croft and a few other individual soothmoothers, who had lived in Shetland for a long time. We hadn't gone very far, when Jill asked the driver to stop.

'That is the oldest hazel tree in the area,' she said proudly, as we hung over a small bridge trying to get a good view of the miniature tree, its fresh greenery overhanging the burn.

'Don't get too excited,' I whispered to Rhys as others rushed to take photos.

'What's that white plant by the burn?' someone asked.

'It's Heath Bedstraw. It has a sickly fragrance.' The soothmoother picked a small sample.

'I would prefer if you didn't pick any of the flowers we see today,' Jill softly scalded.

'What's that Jill?' asked a soothmoother, pointing to a dry grassy place and a low sprawling plant with flowers of bright yellow in leafy clusters.

'Lady's Bedstraw."

'What's that?' asked another. Jill's head twizzled in all directions like a tawny owl.

Poor woman is going to get dizzy if she carries on like this.

'Back in the bus in a few minutes,' she said. 'We have a lot to see and we don't want to miss tea at South Nesting Hall.'

We drove for another ten minutes or so and then we all got out, following Jill like kids pursuing the pied piper of Hamlin.

'Better stay near to Jill if we're going to learn anything,' I said to Rhys in Welsh. I didn't want to be thought pushy; on the other hand Rhys was deaf in one ear.

'Walk near the edge of the field,' said the landowner. 'We have oystercatchers nesting over there.' She pointed to the middle of the field and some low stones. We picked our way carefully noticing different varieties of pink and purple orchids. Jill's patience was endless as she answered and repeated her answers to the hundred's of questions starting with 'What's that?'

It reminds me of going for a walk with the children when they were small. Rhys had the same endless patience to name varieties of flower, butterfly or insect.

I gave up keeping on her tail and wandered off with Rhys, whose knowledge of wild flowers was pretty extensive too. Over the low stone wall and near to the sea was a grassy patch awash with pink campion and sky blue spring squill. The day was brightening up and the cobalt sea looked inviting.

'Do you think I'll ever get to swim in Shetland?' I asked Rhys, straining to hear me.

'What's that?' he answered.

We wandered back to the van and managed to reach South Nesting Hall just in time to enjoy their home bakes and a cup of tea before they closed up at 5pm. Most community halls offered Sunday afternoon teas in summer and they were very popular among locals and tourists. There weren't many cafes in the rural areas, so they served a useful purpose and at the same time raised money for the hall and local charities.

'Have you visited Rosa's garden?' a soothmoother asked me on the way back home in the minibus.

'No, we haven't yet.'

'Then you should. It's looking lovely at the moment.'

I had first noticed brown haired Rosa at the Farmer's Market in Tingwall earlier in the year, selling plants. She was the only woman I had seen in Shetland at the time wearing pink patterned Wellington boots. Then I heard her speak at an Althing debate. She had obviously lived here for a long time, because locals laughed when she referred to herself as a foreigner. 'You're one of us,' another speaker proclaimed. Rosa had a reputation for creating a beautiful garden on the West side over the hill from Weisdale and had recently produced a book called, 'The Impossible Garden.' A few weeks later we went over to have a look. Rosa wasn't there but her partner showed us around. What she had achieved from scratch over a period of twenty years in such a hostile gardening environment was quite extraordinary. There were interesting little walkways and circles around the house with cascades of flowering and aromatic shrubs that we hadn't seen elsewhere in Shetland in such profusion.

'This is a sheltered spot just back from the loch. We planted the sycamores that provide cover and the garden has just evolved,' Rosa's partner said modestly.

'There are some great ideas here. I wish we'd visited earlier in our stay,' Rhys said.

As we drove back along the windswept lochs with their stubby little excuses for trees and back to the empty back garden and lawn of Number 1, Strand Loch, I said to Rhys,
'Well, I think Rosa should have called her book, 'The Remarkable Garden.' It might not be remarkable among the gardens down south but here in the wilds of Shetland it's truly quite remarkable.'

'What! I'm not sure about that,' said Rhys, when I suggested we drop into the Gospel Hall for a talk entitled, Why Jesus Died.' Rhys had been brought up a Methodist with chapel twice on Sunday. His father was a deacon, a pacifist and conscientious objector during the World War 2. He had a hard time because of his beliefs but practised what he preached, However, at a school in Wales where Rhys had taught art, there was a group of evangelical Christians who tried to ram their religion down colleagues' throats and who were critical of those who didn't share their beliefs. While regularly waiting for the bus in the rain these same people would drive by never offering him a lift. Some parallel with the story of the good Samaritan comes to mind.
I had been brought up a Catholic but left the church at 16 on leaving school. I had had enough of feeling guilty about everything that gave me pleasure. Living in southeast Asia I was exposed to and

influenced by other spiritual influences, Islam, Buddhism and Animism, but my political beliefs overrode these for many years. I was with Chairman Mao and Lenin in believing that, 'religion was the opium of the masses,' an ideology that seduced and denied a world outside the body. Over the years that I had known Rhys, we had both moved towards a humanist philosophy. I had dallied with the Quakers for a bit. Rhys believed in the inter-connectedness of the universe as I did and his relationship with nature, rocks and tree roots was the substance of much of his art work before coming to Shetland. As there weren't any tree roots worth painting in Shetland he turned to ancient archaeology for his inspiration. I noticed a shift in us both to a kind of spiritual mysticism.

'Oh come on. We said we'd be open to new experiences,' I urged.

We missed the meeting at the Gospel Hall, but the talk was repeated in a school hall a few miles away the following week.

'There are lots of seats up the front,' a sharp suited young man with a strong Glaswegian accent beckoned, as we entered the small meeting room trying our best not to be noticed. The back two rows were full and there were a handful of other seats occupied.
Not a bad turn out.

The young man was wearing shoes that were so highly polished that they glowed in the dark and he gave an equally polished performance from his laptop, full of colourful flow charts, moving images and slick talk. He didn't quite meet my stereotype vision of a head banger from the Gorbals. We were given shiny folders with a brand new bible, a CD and DVD to take home. It was certainly very different from catechism lessons in school. After an hour he came to a conclusion and said,

'Before I take questions and we break for refreshments, would the ladies mind putting the kettle on?'

The two back rows of ladies rose in unison.
Not such a good turn out then.

We looked at each other recognizing the possible consequences of staying, besides the home bakes, so getting up from our chairs we muttered something about 'another engagement,' 'very interesting,' 'something left on the stove' and other disappointing excuses he must have heard a thousand times before and made for the exit.

'Would you say he had the hwyl?' I asked Rhys in the car.

'Certainly he spoke with conviction and passion, but it's the concept of sin that I find difficult.'

'You mean, that because Jesus was born of a virgin he is not like us sinners, who are stained with the original sin of Adam and Eve?' I asked.

'Yes, it's such a negative start to life. That, and not being allowed to drink alcohol.'

'Oh well, it was interesting, but I'm not ready to go back to organized religion quite yet. Having said that, there's an inter-faith meeting in Lerwick next week, what do you think?'

'Do you fancy a drink?' was the reply.

We didn't make the inter-faith meeting because two things happened. Rhys received a letter from his sister in New Zealand informing him that she had cervical cancer. I checked out with the practice nurse in the Lerwick surgery about the disease and learnt that this was one of those cancers that didn't have a very good recovery rate. Of course without knowing much more she couldn't say but the prognosis would depend on the stage that the cancer was caught. We rang Glenys. She was breathless and in a lot pain and was awaiting an operation to remove litres of fluid in her legs and abdomen.

'I think it's in my bladder too,' she said. Being an ex-nurse she knew what all this could mean.

As we came off the phone Rhys' eyes were red and watery.

'You must go to see her before it gets too bad. At the stage she's at the practice nurse said we shouldn't leave it too long. You should go after we finish here in September,' I said.

'But can we afford it?'

I put my arms around his neck and rubbed my chin against his shiny pebble head.

'Bugger the money. You haven't seen her for eight years. You won't forgive yourself if you never see her again.'

'Perhaps I will get more teaching supply work and sell some pictures before then.'

'Don't worry. You're going.'

'Will you come too?'

'I'm not sure we can afford two tickets. We'll see.'

The second thing that happened was that on the spur of the moment we decided to take a flying visit down sooth. Calum agreed to me taking a couple of days leave tagged onto a weekend, that strictly were not due to the end of my year.

'I know you'll make up the time before then,' he said.

What a boss.

'Jubilant,' is how Rachel described her feeling when we rang and told her from the ferry that we would be arriving the following day. Our very good friend and her adoptive godmother, Elin had been her rock in the past few very difficult months. An ex-teacher and in the educational establishment herself she had been able to give tremendous support and advice on the politics of teaching practice. But Rachel was so pleased to have us there in person. She and I spent a couple of evenings curled up on the sofa talking about our lives and her plans for the future. She was hoping to spend the summer in the French Alps as a chalet host so that she could indulge her hobby of mountain biking and road cycling. She was also starting to look for teaching jobs.

On one day we drove the two and a half hour or so journey up to see Liam at Loughborough, almost the same time it would have taken to have got to Unst from Lerwick. He was in the middle of university exams and struggling, so we took him out for a Sunday roast at a Harvesters. He was keen to talk about the challenges of the year and the future. He didn't know if he would continue into the second year at Uni; to some extent it depended on the exam results. He hoped to spend the summer as a mountain bike guide in Turkey. While we ate he returned several times to the buffet to fill up his plate, which also suggested the trip had been a good idea.

We returned to Shetland a little jaded but pleased that we had been able to offer the children support and ready to make the very most of our last ten weeks on the islands. The weather had perked up from a week ago. When we left it was wet, cold and windy, but now it was fresh, warm and sunny. There were twelve new counselling referrals so I was going to be busy. That was fine. I was becoming more philosophical about the waiting list, trying to focus on the client in the counselling room rather than worrying about the twenty or so folks waiting to see me. I had twenty slots to see clients each week. Much of the work was complex and we still had to do all our own admin. If we increased the number of clients we saw each day we would quickly burn out. We had a system of seeing people quite quickly for assessment so that if there were risk issues regarding their or others' safety these clients could be picked up at an early stage or referred to the community mental health service or alcohol advice service. At assessment we could offer self-help literature and suggestions of work that non-risk clients could do until they saw us for their first appointment. At that point in the year there was a three month waiting list. Considering it was nearly a year in some general practices' down south we were not doing so badly. I did enjoy working with Shetlanders and reminded myself how privileged I was as an incomer to be able to do so.

In my lunch breaks in Lerwick in the better weather I walked along the footpath behind the Health Centre overlooking the island of Bressay. I found a favourite bench slightly out of the wind. It was almost a year since I had come for the interview. It was in that spot I had rung my unsuspecting family with the news. For the next several weeks from that bench I studied the sea in all its lunchtime moods while I dug into the salads that Rhys had prepared for me savouring every moment.

'What do you want for your tea?' Rhys asked, one morning in the middle of June as I got ready for work.
'Oh, something fishy please. Scallops perhaps? And, ah, smoked salmon.'

'Don't you ever get tired of eating smoked salmon?' he laughed.

'Not Shetland smoke salmon. Never.'

'Is it something to do with you being a Cancerian?'

'Maybe, but you know I'm basically just plain greedy when it comes to fish. Remember I wasn't given the nickname Janet the gannet for nothing. I have the girth to prove it. I must have put on over a stone and a half in the last nine months.'

'Ahh. No, you're fine,' he said giving me a cuddle. 'Perhaps I had better not go into McNabs then?'

'I'm not saying that! Can you stock up? Ooh and what about some herrings?'

McNabs was our favourite fishmonger, situated in the harbour by the power station that Gerrie and Joe had recommended to us in the early days of our stay. The elderly owner, a small wiry woman had been a Shetland herring girl in her youth. Shetland, Great Yarmouth and Lowestoft were the top and tail ends of a trade that peaked prior to the First World War. The herring season started in the spring in the north when the herring began their slow annual migration to the southerly breeding grounds of the North Sea. As the herring swam down to the south so the fishermen followed the shoals, from Shetland to Wick, Fraserburgh, Peterhead, South Shields, Scarborough, Great Yarmouth and Lowestoft, taking their biggest catches in the south.

By the mid-19th century a land based mobile work force that could also follow the fishing, with minimum upheaval in working practice, social and familial life, was needed to deal with the catch. Originally, whole families had worked together but by the second half of the 19th century as the industry expanded the women began travelling to gut and pack herring for the large newly-developed curing firms. As they travelled down the east coast of Britain, from port to port, their belongings travelled with them in trunks or kists on special trains from Aberdeen. When not gutting and packing the women knitted. On arrival at the ports the girls, from15 year old virgins to grandmothers in their sixties, stayed in lodgings or bothies, their moral and physical welfare presided over by the Red Cross, the Church of Scotland, the Mission to Fisherfolk, and other religious organizations. What an adventure it must have been for those women!

The industry continued using the herring girls until the 1950's. Opinions as to the decline of the industry include over-fishing by the Danes of immature stock and the decrease in consumption of herring in favour of cod. By the mid-1960's the phenomenon of the herring girls was over.

Days were drawing out and we were moving to mid-summer, the time that Shetlanders call 'simmer dim.' In mid-winter there were less than six hours of daylight; at mid-summer almost eighteen, plus five and a bit hours of surreal twilight - officially referred to as 'civil twilight,' but what was colloquially known as the 'simmer dim.' From mid-May until mid-July the simmer dim gave the midnight hours a magical quality, enhanced by veils of mist swirling up valleys from the sea, making air travel in the mornings unpredictable. On clear nights the light of the simmer dim was enough to read by. It also meant that getting a good night's sleep was difficult.

'What did Calum say about blocking out the light,' Rhys asked that evening, as we sat in the living room eating the McNab scallops that I had gently fried in butter, calorific but sensational.

'He said that there's expensive special curtain lining you can buy, but the cheapskate solution is black bin bags.'

'Shall we try the bin liners first then?' he suggested.

After tea Rhys pulled out a roll of black bin liners, tore them apart and with cellotape made a kind of polythene blind, which he stuck to the window. Then he pulled the curtains.

'What do you think?'

'Not bad, it's not pitch black though.'

'I guess the test will be if we can sleep tonight. Did Calum have any other suggestions?'

'No, but Emily said that scallops are considered an aphrodisiac in Shetland so perhaps we should wait until tomorrow night before we cast judgement.'

What's that smirk, husband?

It was Tuesday, the 21st of June, mid-summer and the longest day of the year. The day started warm and sunny. The sea was a glitterati grey, spangly and sparkling. There had been some mix up over appointments as I had changed my Whalsay/Unst day to Wednesdays from Tuesdays and I had several cancellations in Lerwick. So after I had finished everything I had to do I spent some time internet surfing for flights to New Zealand. We had found out that Glenys, Rhys' sister had stage 3 / 4 cancer. During the operation they removed an ovary, but her womb was stuck to the bowel. It was not good. I found a flight for Rhys for £750 but decided not to book until we had spoken to Glenys again.

When I got back from work Rhys and I discussed what we should do to mark the occasion of mid-summer.

'Maggie told me that traditionally on the longest day people walk up Ronas Hill, the highest spot in Shetland, but the weather looks like it's changing. It's getting colder. I don't feel like getting stuck up there in the mist and rain.'

'No, I agree and it's a long drive. What did Frida tell you about mid-summer's celebrations?'

'She said that you are supposed to celebrate your achievements. You should take along with you something to eat and drink.'

'What about a local walk up to Tronafirth overlooking the sea loch? It's only a half an hour's walk and if the weather changes we can hurry back,' Rhys suggested.

At 9.45pm armed with wine, chocolate, sausages and a small calor gas stove for a barbecue, we strolled up the road to Califf, leaving the road at the top and turning left towards Tronafirth. Jim, our architect friend, had renovated a croft there and the view was magnificent. He didn't mind us walking over his land as long as we took care. His croft was adjacent to another croft that was in disrepair but had grazing for sheep. We had never had any problems wandering across the springy grass down towards the pebbly beach that rimmed the sea loch.

'Oh my God, is it a bull?' I screeched at Rhys.
As I stepped over the gate I was distracted by the view to the left, and on turning I came face to face with a large glossy coated animal. In instances like this Rhys normally reassured me by telling me to look at their nether regions, but I still couldn't tell a male bullock from a female one. However, there was no mistaking that this wasn't a cow and behind him stood his harem of twenty black and white female companions, their Dracula eyes gleaming in the simmer dim.
'I've never seen cattle in this field before,' I muttered.

'Maybe, they bring them to higher ground in the summer, like they do with sheep at home,' Rhys suggested.

'Or do they keep them inside? I can't remember seeing cattle outside in the winter.' 'Well, we can't go that way,' Rhys said, and guided me in the opposite direction to make our descent down a slightly steeper bank.

As we strolled down hand in hand all was quiet and peaceful and I pondered our good luck at having escaped a mid-summer goring. Then suddenly as got nearer the pebbly beach a flurry of nesting artic terns or 'tirricks' as they are known locally because of their specific call, rose up in unison, their privacy invaded by two intruders.

'Oh, bloody hell!'

Time to get going.

'Don't run!' said Rhys, as I simultaneously took flight back up the slope towards Jim's place.

'I've heard they're as aggressive as bonxies and attack by pecking your head with their sharp beaks,' I shouted over my shoulder. I had enjoyed watching tirricks dive bomb for food elsewhere but I had no desire to be dive-bombed myself. I would have worn my cycle helmet if I'd known.

Rhys strolled purposefully behind me. When we reached a safer spot, I said,

'I'm ready for that drink.'

'Aren't we almost in Jim's garden? He may be watching us from his living room window,' Rhys suggested.

'I'm sure he won't mind.' I said, eager for that drink.

Rhys unpacked the picnic and tried to get the fire started hovering behind a small boulder to avoid the wind. It was getting colder and he wasn't having much luck. We decided to abandon the picnic and made our way back home.

'Well, we can certainly list our achievements tonight,' I said, sipping a glass of red in the warmth of the armchair. 'Escaped goring by bull, avoided being flattened by cows and pecked to death by tirricks, and missed out on a sausage barbecue. What do you think Frida would make of that, Rhys?'

'You can ask her,' he said.

'Pardon?'

I turned and saw across the loch our old friend, the white horse, amble down to the water for her night-time tot.

'Cheers, Frida!'

Looking right over Strand Loch

July 2005

'Are you all alright?' I asked my brother John on the phone. It was the evening of July 7th 2005. We had been toying with the idea of going down to Edinburgh for the G8 summit. There was a march and Live 8 concert, 'Making Poverty History,' that Bob Geldof and Bono were hoping would influence world leaders to address the problems in Africa. It would have meant taking another day from the meagre leave I had left so we decided instead to watch the event on TV. What transpired on that day in London is of course also history; a terrorist attack on three tube trains and a bus, at least 50 dead and over 700 people injured. I knew from my days working as a counsellor at Great Western Trains 'injured' in this context didn't mean a few scratched individuals, it meant the loss of limbs and families' futures.

'Yes, we're all o.k. here, fortunately,' John said. He worked for the Daily Mail in South Kensington but travelled across London for business meetings. I rang my cousins and friends, who lived or worked in east London. I even called my stepmother, who rarely ventured east of Earls Court. Everyone was fine but most had a story of someone they knew who had narrowly escaped.

Glenys, Rhys' sister had told us that she thought it would be better if Rhys waited until later on in the year before coming out to New Zealand. She had her children and grandchildren coming to stay. She was feeling a bit better at the moment. 'Come later on in the year, the weather will be better,' she said. We just hoped that 'later on in the year,' would not be too late.

All this put the terrors of bulls, bonxies and tirricks into context.

'Tempus fugit and all that. We need to map out the time we have left here and decide our priorities.' I said to Rhys that week. We got out the map and pinpointed the places we hadn't yet visited; we had done a lot but the list was still long. So we made another list of what was possible; Papa Stour, Mousa (by night), Fair Isle. Oh, and, Out Skerries.

'Yes, he's known to be a bit odd," said Maggie, when we met up with her and Bob for an Indian meal at Raba, one of two Indian restaurants in Lerwick.
'A bit odd? It was like something out of that TV series, 'The League of Gentlemen;' 'a local shop for local people," I answered.

The weather had not looked good as we got on the roll-on roll-off ferry for a day trip to Out Skerries, one of the easternmost of the Shetland Isles, but if we didn't go that weekend in July it was hard to see how we were going to fit it in. We started off on top watching the landslip by, but after a while a light rain started and the crew insisted we go below and sit in the small warm lounge to while away the couple of hours to our destination.

Out Skerries consist of three small islands and a number of skerries, small uninhabited rocks dotted around them. The main islands of Bruray (Bridge Isle) and Housay (House Isle) have long been joined by a bridge. Grunay (Green Island) forms the south eastern side of the harbour. Coming into the harbour there was a fine lighthouse, built in 1858 but automated in 1972. In World War 2 German planes made several low level attacks, one of which killed a keeper's wife. A British aircraft on its way back from a raid on Norway crash-landed on Grunay, with the loss of the three crew.

The population was very small, around 60 people and because of a shortage of water most of the houses were gathered near to the harbour as water has to be frequently shipped in. Despite its size there was a primary school, which had been the subject of much debate. The Shetland Islands Council was looking to balance its budget and the school was a target for a proposed cut. However, the local councillor with the support of the population had managed a stay of execution. The teacher and GP were flown in by Loganair.

When we arrived we decided to do a quick tour of the island by car to get a feel for it and then wrap up warm and have a walk. The return ferry would leave around 4pm so we had a few hours to enjoy the place. The quick tour of the island was quick; perhaps five minutes or was it four and a half? That left four hours

for walking - in the rain. It was July but the temperature was probably around 8degrees, but rain had never put us off before, so we parked the car by the harbour and set off in an anti-clockwise direction. There were lots of wild flowers; flowers that would have been blooming in May at home like sea thrift, and ox-eye daisies were rampant. There were lots of other varieties that we didn't recognize.
Note to self; buy a book on local wild flowers.

    We had heard that there were otters to be seen on Out Skerries and as the total Shetland otter population had managed to avoid us so far in our stay, we were determined not to miss out on this trip. We walked across an ancient system of 'rigs', where arable land was divided into strips and cultivated in rotation. Stepping through the long wet grass was pleasant for its lush springy quality but I could feel water creeping into my boots. I began to squelch.

    'Could that be a place for otters?' I asked Rhys, pointing to a flat rocky area by the sea.

    'Could be,' he said.

    We squelched on.

    'Could that be?' I asked again, pointing to something else similar.

    'Could be.'

    'Why don't we ask someone?'

    There didn't seem to be anyone round to ask. As soon as we saw someone emerge from their house, they seemed to scurry away like a frightened dormouse in Alice in Wonderland. We stepped over a wooden gate and found that we were quite near the harbour. Fishing was important to Out Skerries folk, and judging by the size of some of their homes, they seemed to be making a good living out of it. There had been a community salmon farm at one time but declining market prices had affected its future.

We came across a sign 'Fresh eggs for sale.'
That would be nice for tea.

Several brown hens clucked around Rhys's feet as I pushed him towards the door.

He rang the bell. He rang the bell again but there was no answer.

'Where is everybody?' Rhys asked, then surrounded by about thirty cluckers.
Taste the fresh yellow yoke. Yummy.

He tried a final time.

'No luck. Shall we go? Why have a sign if you don't open the door?' Rhys asked.

'Well, it is tipping it down. Where do you think most people are on a miserable wet Saturday afternoon? I know where I would prefer to be.'

'I see what you mean.'

Then as we wandered into the harbour I saw the sign, 'Shop'. We hadn't seen it before because we had walked in an anti-clockwise direction away from the harbour.

Oh great! Maybe there's a café with a roaring fire we can sit by for the next two and a half hours.

'Is it open?' Rhys asked.

At that moment a young man came out of the door clutching a bottle of lemonade. I remembered I had seen him scurrying away earlier. Then an older man followed him out holding a bag of potatoes. I recognized him from the colour of his anorak.

We entered the porch and I understood. There was a notice with the shop times; on Saturdays it seemed the shop was only open for a couple of hours in the afternoon and not open on Sundays. Locals were just stocking up before the shop closed for the weekend. So, we were not in a surreal fairy story after all. Well, that was what I thought momentarily until we entered the shop.

It was dark and it took a little time for our eyes to get accustomed to the gloom. The radio was on loud. It sounded like the Test match coming live straight from the Oval in Kennington.

If I was at the Oval could I imagine that there was still a place like this in 21st century Britain? Probably not.

I looked around. The shop seemed to be divided into two halves, one was stone built, the other could have been wood and brick. It seemed more the kind of place you might have kept animals. There was the most curious collection of goods on sale. Some of the wrappings looked like they were from the 1950s; the sort you would find in a folk museum like Beamish or St. Fagan's - Eccles cakes, Vim and Marmite. Then I wandered into the other half of the shop. There were several shelves packed ceiling to floor with toys, some

looked like Christmas leftovers and some possibly of the blow up variety.
Right.

'Have you seen a shopkeeper?' I asked Rhys, who was looking through an old collection of postcards.

'No,' he said. 'Have you seen the chocolate?'

'I think I saw bars of Frys, 'Five Boys' back there.'
Difficult to say 'Go and see the sex toys,' without being overheard.

Then I saw a plump little man with his head down in an exercise book, doing his accounts by the look of things.

'Do you know where we could see the otters?' I asked.

'No.'
Don't look up then.

'We're closing soon. Is it just the Eccles cake you wanted?'

Rhys put a couple of postcards on the table and a bar of Cadbury's whole milk chocolate. He spied a brightly coloured packet of fishing flies. He pulled it off the rack and put it on the table.

'Aren't they beautiful colours?' he said to the top of the man's head.
I don't think he's an artist, Rhys.

'No 'Five Boys' then?' I asked.

'What?' He looked at me curiously.

'Do you know where we could possibly see otters?' Rhys repeated.

When the man told us the price of the few items, we looked at each other askance, but I decided not to ask for a breakdown. We left, went back to the car and squelched down in the seats. We were soaked through. The rain was so heavy we could hardly see out of the steamed up window.

'What if it's too rough for the ferry to come and pick us up?' I said.

Is that panic in your eyes, Rhys bach?

'Better break the Eccles into smaller pieces then.' he replied.

'No, I'm not going to the Lerwick practice barbecue,' I told Tracy in a break between our clients.

'It would be good for public relations.'

'I am sorry Tracy, but it's ten months too late for me.'

'It would build bridges.'

'Yes, I can see that and it is important for you and the Service, but I think my anger at the lack of their personal interest in us over the year would spill out. Also, I don't want to have to explain and repeat to all of them why I'm leaving.'

'Well, if you change your mind, give us a call. I'll probably pop in for an hour or so.'

'You're still angry?' Freya asked at our next art therapy session.

'I suppose I am. You come a thousand miles to a different culture. There are maybe two or three other people here who speak your language. Don't you think it's rather mean and odd to show no interest in those people?'

I was referring in particular to the one Welsh speaking doctor in Shetland, who was my colleague in Lerwick, who even had the Welsh national anthem hanging on his wall in the surgery, but answered me in English, when I attempted in my learner's tongue to be friendly. Rhys's first language was Welsh and he would have loved an opportunity to speak to a native speaker, but the GP had kept his distance.

'Well, I guess folk have their reasons,' Freya said, non-judgementally.

'Yes, perhaps he doesn't want to be associated with the past. He's pretty well settled here. But, I think what this throws up for me yet again, Freya, is that I still seem to think I'm entitled to be looked after by other people, people who owe me nothing.'

'That abandoned needy child again?'

'Yep, I need to give her a good talking to.'

'Siarad Cymraeg?' Rhys asked a young man on the street in Lerwick. It was the start of the 'Island Games,' and he had spotted a guy wearing an 'Ynys Mon' T shirt.

'Pardon?'

'Sorry, I thought you must be from Anglesey, wearing the T shirt.'

'No mate, I'm one of the few people in Anglesey who don't speak Welsh. But I can tell you where you will find someone who does.'

It was mid-July and Lerwick had increased its population threefold. There were athletes from islands as far apart as the Falklands, Rhodes, Iceland, and the Isle of Man. There were dozens of islands I had never heard of, most of them seemingly from somewhere in the Baltic. Shetland was hosting the Island Games this year and the Council had gone all out to make sure people had a good time. The streets were lined with bunting and there was a carnival atmosphere. Most people we knew were involved in some way or other, stewarding at events or hosting folk in their homes. Emily was stewarding at the squash events, because her son Jamie was in the Shetland squad. He represented Scotland at a high level.

'Prynhawn da,' Rhys said, as he entered the Ynys Mon cyclists' tent at Tingwall Junior School, just over the wall from us at Strand Loch. A lycraed figure replied,

'Good afternoon. Rydych chi a'r gwyliau yma? Are you on your holidays?'

'Na. Rwy'n byw yma. I live here.'

'Pam mae Cymro Cymraeg yn byw yma.? Why is a Welsh speaking man living up here?'

'Gee, mae'n wyllt yma. Wow, it's wild here. I couldn't live here. And I thought Anglesey was quiet. It's too quiet for me.'

It was a bit of luck for Rhys. All the cycling events started from our window. Island flags sang their anthems in the wind. Or perhaps it was the flag posts. It was very windy. Rhys filled in the cyclists from Ynys Mon on our history. A perfect opportunity to get his tongue round his Welsh mutations with born Welsh speakers and catch up with what was happening in the land of his fathers.

We looked in on a number of other events throughout the week, athletics and volleyball, but we missed seeing Emily's son do well in his squash events. On Friday, it was the final in the football. Shetland was playing Guernsey for the cup. The match was in the park next door to Montfield, and Calum's boss was playing in this special event. As it was admin day, Calum suggested I take an extended lunch break to go watch. I wandered out, looking for Tracy.

Perhaps she can tell me the rules.

The park was packed with other people taking extended lunch breaks. It looked like the whole population of Lerwick had come out to cheer-on the Shetland side. The atmosphere was electric. I sat on a wall for a while until a gang of large Island Game competitors from Gotland stood in front of me and blocked my view. So I decided to wander into town about half a mile away. It was absolutely empty. Everyone was at the game and you could hear their cheers from the Pier Head. I hadn't missed out though. I took a seat on the pier and watched the televised version on the big screen. The final result? A victory for

Shetland and even better for the counselling service, a winning goal was scored by Calum's boss.
Now he's in a good mood, time to ask for more admin support, Calum.

'Call me at 9pm and I'll tell you if we're on. It looks like the weather may be with us,' said Tom Jamieson, skipper of Solan IV, the boat taking visitors to the small island of Mousa, off the south-east coast of Shetland. Earlier in the season we had visited the island during the day and seen blubbery barking seals protecting their young, porpoises playing in the harbour and bonxies in waiting, alert to new birth, ready to pluck out the eyes of their prey. But coming to Mousa at night was going to be very different.

At half past eleven in mid-July, 60 degrees north, Tom Jamieson ferried thirty excited twitchers across the water from Sandwick heading for Mousa in search of the storm petrel. The oceans of the world are home to the petrels. They go ashore only to breed or when driven by the storms. But it takes a storm of more than ordinary fury to get the better of these birds. They shelter from the Atlantic gales by keeping to the troughs of waves and avoiding the crests. They silently follow boats and feed off plankton, crustaceans and small fish. On calm days they often patter over the surface of the water as if walking. The name 'petrel' is said to have been derived from the biblical episode on which St Peter walked on the water. Since around that time and ever since, each summer thousands have flocked to the island of Mousa to nest and breed in the stones of its ancient broch. They fly into their hotel at dusk and out at dawn a few hours later in search of breakfast.

We stepped off the ferry into the fading violet light and followed Tom's son, Stuart in single file along the shoreline towards the broch.

'Can ye hear them? They only make this sound at night or on the nest. Come closer,' he beckoned and the pushy types huddled round him as he put his ear to the low stone boundary wall. We could hear a faint purring, churring and clucking, but could see nothing. Meanwhile those in the know hurried on towards the broch, the best preserved in Scotland.

'Look!' said Rhys.

The massive circular fortress with its dry stone walls rose like an industrial cooling tower waiting patiently for its night time visitors. This broch was built around 100BC-100AD, a fortress for Vikings seeking shelter. An outside diameter of twenty meters and a height of over fifteen, its base is hollow with stone lintels tying the walls together. The tiny spaces between the stones provide a warm dry place for 'stormies,' as the locals call them, to bunk down for the night.

I like watching and hearing birds, but given my early childhood budgie trauma my worst nightmare would be to be stuck in a room with a frightened bird in flight.

The light was fading fast now. The atmosphere eerie, mysterious, expectant. Then in the dark silence we heard a distant - 'arrrr-r-r chick-a', and something flew close to my face. It looked like a bat and I clung onto Rhys' sleeve as if he was going to be able to protect me from 6,000 of these treasures.

'Do stormies have radar?'

'Not sure,' he said absentmindedly, his heart focused on the experience of the moment. Slowly, first, one by one, then a few at a time, then more, then maybe fifty, a hundred, five hundred, a thousand, three thousand, six thousand sooty bombers darted in from the sea behind us at all angles homing in on their individual hotel rooms.

'Are you coming in?' Rhys asked as he crouched down to move into the entrance to the broch. 'Tom has found one in a hollow and is shining a light on the bird to show us what they look like close up.'

'Maybe not,' my fight-flight response already in overdrive.

'It would be a shame to have come this far and not see one close up.'

Rhys took my moist hand. My heart felt as if it was about to pop through my chest like Sigourney Weaver giving birth to the Alien, and my mouth tasted like a sour lemon. I ducked down into the low entrance. There it was, small, unassuming, and apparently unafraid. The very opposite of me. It couldn't hurt anything. A storm petrel weighs only 26grams, about the same as a house sparrow. It appears all black but has a white rump and a short white bar on the under wing. It resembles a house martin.

'Stormies have one egg, white with faint brown spots, incubation is 38-43 days, young fledge at 59-75 days,' said our guide.

'How can such a tiny creature fly all the way to Africa and back each year?' I asked, trying distraction as a way of overcoming my irrational fear.

'It's extraordinary, isn't it? And some have been known to live for over twenty years." said Tom, his grey beard pearly in the upward reflection of his torchlight.

As we sailed away back towards Sandwick the night enveloped Mousa's secret into its silky embrace.

'How do you feel? Rhys asked, giving my hand a squeeze. 'Do you think you've conquered your fear of flying birds?'

No!

'Time will tell I suppose.'

I stared back into the pitch. 'Good night, stormies. Sleep tight.'

Friday July 15th. It was my birthday. Was I really 57years old? Wasn't 57 the new 47? That didn't sound much better. I felt somewhere deep inside just 27. But I did feel very happy. It had been such an interesting and demanding year. Although I still wasn't fully able to tame my angry and needy inner child, I felt more energised and focused, more self-aware and more connected to the landscape, nature and the sea. Rhys and I had become closer because of our experience and

I had fallen in love with him all over again. There was so much to celebrate. Now, was time to start to look to the future. What next?

Frida, my friend and ex-colleague had left the Royal College of Nursing almost a year before after ten years working there and set herself up in private practice. She had some regular clinical supervision with nurses in the NHS, which provided some core income, and she was registered with some employee assistance agencies for counselling referrals. She also had a very good website designed by a close friend that was a source of further work.

'Do you know what? I think I'd like to try and do what Frida's done this year,' I said to Rhys that evening as I stuffed my birthday face with fresh smoke salmon.
'What has she done this time?'
'You know, set herself up in private practice. I would still need a core part-time job. Perhaps they would take me back at Gwent Family Mediation?'
'I don't think you should take on too much.'
'No, I would have to be careful about doing that. I'm just a bit concerned about how we'd manage financially.'
'Well, when we go back hopefully I will get more teaching supply work and sell some pictures.'
Yes, when have I heard that before?

Rhys' supply work in Shetland had dried up because it was the school summer holidays. His touring exhibition of Shetland's archaeology had been much admired throughout the islands but there were no sales. The gallery organizing these exhibitions did not really promote them in the island venues. Their aim seemed to be more about raising awareness of the arts rather than selling. The gallery put its best promotional efforts into selling at its main space, the Bonhoga. We had joined as friends and been to several previews. It was a light airy space and there was an interesting programme of work from locals and foreigners.

'Have you heard anything about the post cards?'

'No, I'm not sure what's happening at Old Scatness. I must ring them again.'

Rhys had some landscape pictures in several small galleries in Lerwick; the Health craft gallery, the Harbour gallery, the Vaila, and the Norwegian Café. He had taken a stall to sell his work at the Tingwall Farmer's market on one occasion, and had work on display in the 'Veer North' stand at the summer festival on Victoria Pier.

'Veer North' was a group of visual artists living in Shetland cooperatively promoting their own work. We didn't know how successful they were, but the standard of work was very high. There were some outstanding artists, including Howard Toull, who was a countryside ranger and whose pictures of birds shot across the paper, full of vitality, and Ruth Brownlee, whose seascapes are bold, splashing wild spume out at the viewer. Rhys had joined this group and had been out sketching with some of them. He had tried his best to promote his own work, without wishing to be seen as the over-pushy foreigner. There had been interest but very few sales. The worst summer weather-wise in Shetland since 1942 didn't help sales either.

The exception to all of this was the Archaeology Department of the Amenities Trust. Val Turner, the principal archaeologist had given Rhys permission to sketch and paint on site at Scatness Iron Age village. Old Scatness Broch and its associated wheelhouses was first discovered during road-building in 1975. Together with Jarlshof and Mousa it was one of the most important sites in Shetland. Scatness was thought to have been continuously occupied for 2,500 years. The lowest levels of the broch had been dated to somewhere between 400 and 200BC, whilst the surrounding aisled wheelhouses date from 100BC. Replicas of various houses had been built next to the site and exhibitions about stone working, spinning, weaving, beer making and other Iron Age activities are on display. The staff even dressed in historic costume, which in a bad summer must have been somewhat chilly.

Val had bought six of Rhys' pictures that went on sale in the Scatness shop. There didn't seem to be any other artist doing work of this sort. She also mentioned the possibility of publishing post-cards of his work but he was still waiting on a decision about funding. It's hard to keep motivated as an artist when you're not selling and many artists are not that good at self-promotion. Rhys had been tremendously well disciplined that year and produced some very good work. I wanted to be encouraging and supportive as I believed in his talent but I was also a realist. Sadly, he was now of an age, when to employ him as a supply teacher in Wales was too expensive for most schools. It seemed that they preferred inexperienced younger teachers because they were cheaper to employ. Unless you were a Tracey Emin or a Damien Hurst any artist would find it difficult to live by their art alone. The consequence and reality of this for me was that although Rhys was in receipt of a small pension, I would need to continue to carry the main financial burden in our relationship.

Towards the end of July, the news broke that RAF Saxavord in Unst would be cut shortly, meaning the loss of over 100 jobs and more people lost to the community. People had suspected this would happen at some point but not without a reasonable lead-in time. The immediacy of the decision could have a huge impact on the local economy and on the status of the school, transport and the health service there. I was working in Unst on the 26th and the mood was low. However, as ever, Emily in a reply to an e-mail I sent, kept an optimistic stance.

'The island has been dependent on the RAF for such a long time. Perhaps their going presents us with an opportunity.'
I hope so Emily. I really hope so.

Inside Mousa Broch

August 2005

'Is that one coming or going?' I asked Rhys one afternoon in early August. Looking at his watch without hesitation he replied,

'Returning from Papa Stour, I would think.'

His studio in the utility room didn't have many advantages. It was very small and cramped; his drawing board rested on the freezer and gave him frozen knees and the washing machine on a full cycle didn't help his tinnitus. However, there was a large window, from where he could watch the wind turbines in the far distance, but more importantly for him it was the perfect place to observe planes.

Tingwall Airport was just half a mile away. Loganair's 8 seater plane, 'The Islander,' transported folk daily to and from Foula, Fair Isle, Out Skerries and Papa Stour. The pilot didn't know it but he was Rhys's one reliable companion each day; that was unless it was too foggy or the weather was bad and then flights were cancelled often at very short notice.

Rhys loves heights. When I first met him we could be walking in the country, when suddenly he would disappear and then would call me from the top of a large oak tree, hanging upside down from a high branch like a lemur. His antics climbing on high cliffs left me jelly like at the bottom warning him to be careful. Rhys also loves flying. He was always excited whenever we travelled by plane. He wasn't an anorak exactly. It was seeing the world from above, from a different angle, that really inspired him. You could see that in his rocks and roots pictures. He painted nature from unexpected vantage points.

'Well, I have a special treat for you.'

'No, you have the last of the salmon. I've had enough.'

'No silly, not that. I'm going to treat you to a trip on the Islander.'

He flushed.

'What about you? Wouldn't you like to come?'

'I would like to but it may be difficult to arrange. I can't take any more time off.' Calum 's been brilliant but I don't want to take advantage. With the weather being so wintry and there being a very limited weekend schedule you may have to go on your own in the week. Would that be o.k.?'

'Yes, but... I'd feel guilty going without you.'

'No buts. Where would you like to go?'

'Well, we've been to Out Skerries, we're going by boat to Papa Stour this weekend and to Fair Isle later this month on the Good Shepherd, so what about Foula?'

'O.K. I'll leave it to you to book.' But he wasn't listening. He was already somewhere over the Atlantic way up in the clouds.

That Saturday we got up early and drove towards Aith on the West side. We had chartered a boat, a small leisure cruiser to take us around Papa Stour. The guidebook told us that 'it had perhaps the best cliff scenery in Shetland or even the UK... in settled weather an exploration by boat is said to be quite exceptional. The red cliffs are formed from volcanic rhyolite which have eroded into a fantastic series of stacks, caves, arches, geos and skerries. Basalt and Old Red Sandstones underlie the rhyolite and it is a Special Area of Marine Conservation.'

Papa Stour, which means in Old Norse, 'the Large Isle of the Priests,' refers to Celtic missionaries who lived there perhaps as early as the 6th century. With a landlocked safe harbour at Hamna Voe and a strategic position on the west coast of the islands it became an important Viking base.

The island had come to our attention in the early days of our stay in Shetland through the pages of the Shetland Times. The population was small, perhaps 40 people. It seemed that there was an on going feud between two families; the father of one of the families was also 'a father' to the rest of the islanders. The latest incident in the winter of 2004 involved horse and dog ownership. It seemed that a Shetland pony owned by the minister's wife had been worried by a dog from another croft, resulting in the minister shooting the dog. The Shetland Times, told us that, 'the dog belonged to one of the minister's enemies in the community.' The case went to court and he was acquitted, but called for a police enquiry, vowing 'to continue living there despite the bitter feuding that characterises the community.' The Shetland Times added, 'he is writing a book about his life since leaving the outskirts of Bournemouth.'

Sounds like good material for the libel courts.

The east end of Papa Stour was very fertile and supported a wide variety of plants; that is where all the inhabitants lived; over the centuries most of the west end had been used to provide fuel, turfs for rooves, to improve the crofts, and as bedding for animals. In the 1960s and 70's Papa Stour attracted hippy types looking for an alternative life style. There were mixed feelings about this from Shetlanders we spoke to. Some believed that without them life on the island would have died, others that they were spongers on social security and the lowest form of life. Even with a ferry and mains electricity the economy today was said to be 'fragile'.

'The guide book says that, 'on foggy summer days fishermen could find their way home by following the scent of the wild flowers,' I quoted, as we mooched towards the island in our chartered boat. Another couple who had booked didn't turn up so we had the owner and the boat with its tiny cabin all to ourselves.

'Mmm, how lovely,' Rhys said, sniffing the air.

It took some time to get very far, and as we slipped along the west coast of the mainland, the skipper pointed out land marks on the way; Ronas Hill, in the distance, the relics of old guns from the wars, remains of ancient brochs, good places to fish etc. The day started quite well, it was warm and sunny but by the time we reached West Burrafirth, from where the ferry left the mainland for the island, the weather had changed and it was a choppy ride across the sound.

White spume parted as the boat's prow bobbed along, parallel to the coast of the island.

'Can you get any nearer?' asked Rhys, who had dreamt of sailing into 'Kirstan's Hole,' where a cave had partially collapsed to form a gloup. The pictures in the guidebook looked awesome.

''Fraid not, it's too dangerous with the weather changing.'

The skipper continued to plough his boat along the coast of Papa Stour in an anti-clockwise direction. It started to rain but through the mist we still had great views of the stacks, the geos, small caves and the Old Red Sandstone cliffs at the far west end of the island. As we came around along the north coast up to the east side of Papa Stour we caught sight of the tiny harbour and the few homesteads.

'It must be hell living in such an isolated spot and be in such conflict with your neighbours,' I said.
The skipper remained diplomatically silent. Seeing our disappointment at not getting into the caves, he asked,

'Do you like fishing?'

Rhys' face brightened. He explained about his unsuccessful attempts at fishing with his barber.

'Look on the satellite, there's mackerel nearby.' He pointed at a visual device in front of him with lots of blue and red splodges moving around.

I'll take your word for it, Skip. I had the same problem when I was pregnant seeing a baby at 16 weeks on the ultrasound. That splodge inside me could have been mackerel for all I could make out.

We left Papa Stour behind and the skipper nudged his boat up to the mackerel feeding ground off the west coast of the mainland. He pulled out a fishing line with lots of hooks on it. He cast it out and we waited. And waited. And waited. He pulled it out, but no luck. He cast again and again and again.

'No luck here,' he said, and moved the boat a few hundred metres. He repeated this manoeuvre three times.

'You can't leave without taking something home for your supper,' he said and cast again.
You Shetlanders, you'll go to such lengths to make folk happy, but the mackerel have moved on, as we need to. I'm starving.

Finally, after a few more attempts he pulled up the multi hook from the water and there was one little mackerel attached. The skipper smiled and pulled it off.

'It's not much, but take it,' he said, wrapping the wee thing up in some old Shetland Times.
No Skip, you take it. You deserve it. Full marks for perseverance.

'This year's been a bad year for fishing,' he added.
Now, where have I heard that before?

'Let us drive back via Sandness. There might be a shop or a pub there,' I suggested to Rhys as we left the skipper and made for the car. The community shop in Aith was closed, but after all this time I still naively expected there to be other places open in the area selling food and drink on a late Saturday evening in the height of summer.

'No luck,' he said, coming back from the public toilet. We had parked in a hamlet called Melby, a tiny harbour facing the south coast of Papa Stour.

'Why not? Wouldn't you expect to find food and drink on sale in a public toilet?'

'No, it's the building; it looked promising.'

'Would you look in the back of the car, just in case there's something edible that's hiding?'

'Sure.'

Rhys came back with a bruised apple, a few toffees and some broken biscuits. We sat in the car and munched our way through them. The weather was changing and we were enjoying watching it pass across the sound as we had done on the boat a few hours earlier.

'What on earth are <u>they</u> doing?'

While Rhys had gone to the loo I had my eyes behind the binoculars scanning Papa Stour in the distance, the Sound, and back to Melby, admiring the swathes of ox-eye daisie, large white and yellow daisies fringing the shore, and zooming in on the flotsam and jetsam on the beach in case I saw something to eat.

Anyone would think I hadn't eaten for weeks.

I had seen a couple of men pulling out a small boat, like a rowing boat, from the stone building that housed the public toilet. An Asian woman with a mane of long black hair pulled two very large suitcases out of a parked car and dragged them towards the concrete landing spot. The men got the boat into the water, put the suitcases and other bags in and the three of them jumped in. The small boat rocked. It was low in the water and didn't look very safe.

'They're not going across the Sound to Papa, are they? Look the rain is getting heavier, the clouds are darkening. It looks like a real storm is brewing.'

'They are. There's a trail of blue smoke from the outboard motor.'

It was very unusual to see an Asian woman in Shetland especially on the West side.
Standing in a small boat in a storm without a life jacket? Not for much longer either.

'Do you think she's an illegal immigrant?' Rhys joked.

'No, she's more likely to be the new minister. The old one left a few weeks ago. He had a great farewell. As he got on the ferry his sworn enemy threw a bucket of dogs' poo over him.'
Good Luck my lovely!

'Oh no, she's not the new minister,' grinned Pete, an organic crofter and friend of Gerrie and Joe, who along with his wife, a couple of folk dancers and ourselves had been invited over to Gruting for a dinner party. Gerrie had once been a chef and we had really been looking forward to the evening.

'She works for the Centre,' he said as we enjoyed our pre-dinner drinks in the large living room.

'Centre?' I asked.

'Centre for addicts. She's gone over to help for a few weeks. She definitely survived the boat trip; we were with her this morning at the Peerie Café in Lerwick.'

Small world.

'It's a great place for recovery and rehabilitation,' said Gerrie, filling our wine glasses. 'There's no alcohol or drugs allowed. People pay their way by helping out on the croft, on the land or with the animals. They do some super work.'

'Not an illegal immigrant or new minister then? A social worker, perhaps?' I said.

'You have to be careful. That's the way rumours spread,' laughed Gerrie, and quickly changing the subject, turned to the folk dancers and asked,

'You remember Janet and Rhys, don't you? They came dancing with us to your Waas class one evening last year.'

'Oh yes, very well,' the woman replied. I saw the lines around her eyes pucker and I cringed as we eyed each other in simultaneous recognition.

What did you say about spreading rumours, Gerrie?

'No, I'm not a social worker, I'm an agronomist,' replied the shiny black haired woman at dinner in the Bird Observatory on Fair Isle a few weeks later.

'And you're not Asian?'

'Asian? No. I'm Canadian, working my way across Europe. I do farm and croft sits, while farmers have a holiday. It's difficult for many to get away because looking after someone else's land and animals is a big responsibility. You need someone who you can trust and who is qualified.'

I related my fantasy about her and her boat trip to Papa Stour.

'We were worried that in the small boat in the brewing storm you wouldn't survive. We were on the verge of alerting the life boat.'

'Yes, I remember seeing someone looking at me through binoculars. Were you in a dark green Estate?' *Wonder what your fantasy is about what I was doing? I can see the headline in the Shetland Times - 'Counsellor found guilty on Peeping Tom charges.'*

'Yes, it's a small world, isn't it? Can I take your plate?'

We had been looking forward to coming to Fair Isle all year. As a small child I had worn the traditional patterned gloves made in Fair Isle and fashionable in the 1950s. To promote the knitting industry in the 1920s the Prince of Wales had set a trend among golfers sporting Fair Isle waistcoats and pullovers at Royal events. In the early 1950s the fashion eventually found its way down to the English working class, who if they couldn't afford the original item bought the intricate patterns and knitted the beautiful hats, gloves and sweaters themselves.

'The Shipping Forecast' on late night radio, was the other influence urging me to visit the island. How often had I lain in bed cosy and warm and wondered about the nation's fishermen in gale Force 10s catching the cod and haddock for Friday night's supper? 'Fair Isle, Faroes and Iceland,' was at the end of the forecast and always filled my imagination with remote imagery and romantic ideas.

'I've never been to Fair Isle. I'd love to come,' responded Gerrie, when I asked if she and Joe would like to join us for a couple of days in late August.
'But I'm a terrible sailor, so if we come we'll fly.'

'It may be better up top in the fresh air if you can't sleep,' suggested Neil Thompson, the second in command on the Good Shepherd IV, the boat that regularly ferried locals and tourists from Grutness, near Sumburgh on the south mainland to Fair Isle. The journey was around three hours and had a reputation for challenging the stomachs of even the best sailors due to the strong currents and tides between the mainland and Orkney. Fair Isle in August was often beset by mist, meaning that the small inter-island plane, The Islander, didn't fly and so it was that Gerrie and Joe found themselves up top with Rhys and I sailing south.

'What did Woody Allen say about the middle bit of eternity being the longest?' Neil said helpfully as he lent over us to see how we were all doing. Neil had been Gerrie's first husband's best man at their wedding and they hadn't seen each other for some time.

'I'm feeling a bit nauseous,' said Gerrie snuggling up beside me over the vibrations of the engine.

It was chilly and we were sheltering from a light drizzle.

'How's Joe doing?' asked Neil. We all looked over to Joe, his face as pale as a codfish, his head and shoulders stooped, his knuckles clenched on two parallel bars as if he was getting ready to do a fancy gymnastic move.

'I'm alright as long as I don't move,' a voice mumbled from under Joe's parker hood.

Rhys stood for most of the trip, half in the control cabin, with the skipper, crew and locals who chatted in dialect about the state of the world, and half out on deck enjoying the fresh air.

'I think we'll be taking 'The Islander' back,' said Gerrie emphatically, as we all wobbled off at North Haven. The Good Shepherd IV unloaded its cargo by crane. Off came large quantities of bottled water that was essential back up to the island's own natural supplies, boxes and small containers. We watched as a car was expertly picked up like a soft toy in a fairground game and placed neatly on the quayside.
Neil must have won a lot of furry bunnies for his children over the years.

There was no hierarchy on the Good Shepherd. It was all hands on deck. The Skipper put on his overalls and helped the crew with unloading. Sometimes the Good Shepherd itself had to be hauled out of the water between trips because of the exposed situation of the new breakwater and pier.

A minibus from the Bird Observatory was there to meet us at the quayside and took us the quarter of a mile up to the Centre which was to provide us with comfortable shelter and excellent food for the next couple of days.

Fair Isle or 'Frideray' in Old Norse lies mid-way between Sumburgh Head and North Ronaldsay in Orkney. The island became famous in the early 20th Century for pioneering studies on bird migration, and the Bird Observatory established in 1948 by George Waterson remained a very important part of its economy. The island lies on the main migration routes from Iceland, Greenland and Scandinavia to Britain. At least 359 species have been observed on Fair Isle, of which 45 are regular breeders. Over 320,000 birds had been ringed and released over the years, and between April and mid-August the island is a twitcher's paradise.

We were offered a high tea of toast and homemade cake to settle our stomachs. After eating, the Warden's wife gave us a welcome spiel, telling us the house rules, such as using the boot room for outdoor gear and using the honesty box for buying alcohol. It all sounded and felt very laid back. The young woman talked about the guided walks and the nightly entertainment. She then gave us all a map and showed us the places of interest, pointing out that we

could walk almost anywhere; 'almost' excluded one croft and small area of land. She didn't elaborate but insisted that we didn't trespass there.
Wonder if that's because of some local feud?

Afterwards we went for a stroll. The island is only 3 miles long with the Bird Observatory in the north and the museum, churches and most of the island homes in the more fertile south. The Observatory had a paid warden and his wife, a cook and an assistant, and a number of summer volunteers, mainly young people who helped with ringing and recording migratory birds, nursing injured ones and doing any necessary conservation and renovation work to the Centre.

Apart from the volunteers and our Canadian 'friend', our fellow guests at the Observatory included a crew of heavies working for the Water Authority and doing work on the Northern Lighthouse, a spattering of binoculared booted pensioners, and an Italian couple; Carla, the wife, who was a history teacher with a passion for textiles and her husband Paulo, an ex-teacher with an interest in creative photography.

We walked towards the northern lighthouse. There were two lighthouses on the island, another one in the south. They were both built in 1892 by the Stevensons, partly to assist the Royal Navy and partly to stem the number of shipwrecks. The southern lighthouse was the last to be automated in Scotland in 1998.

'Aren't lighthouses romantic?' I said to Gerrie as we walked around the northern lighthouse.

'You should talk to Neil about that. He and his father were lighthouse keepers here for a long time.'

'It's like a Kapoor sculpture," I said, scanning my hand over the huge maroon bassoon in front of the light stack.

'It's the fog siren,' Joe said, bringing logic back into the conversation. 'German aircraft often attacked lighthouses in World War 2. The wives of two keepers were killed at the southern lighthouse.'

'Shall we get going? We don't want to be late for supper,' Gerrie said.

So we turned round and made our way back to the Observatory. We passed a small loch, where we spotted a few birds we thought we recognized, so on our return to the Centre Gerrie picked up the red felt tipped pen and wrote the species, the spot where we had seen them, and the approximate numbers on the wipe clean board used for the purpose in the lounge.

'That's interesting,' said the warden, watching her in full felt tipped flow. He moved forward and discretely commented,

'Dunlins aren't usually found in that part of the island. Are you sure they were dunlins?' After a good humoured discussion Gerrie wiped our red lettered observations off the board.

'Better leave it to the experts,' Joe joked as Gerrie joined the rest of us for a pre-supper drink in the lounge.

After supper we sat in the lounge waiting for the entertainment. But before it could begin there was a

special ritual, the bird count. There was a 'Sshh' as the warden sat down and opened a large ledger, the log. Absolute silence prevailed as in alphabetical order he read out the names of birds you could expect to see at that time of the year. People in the audience were invited to stop him if they had seen a particular species, say the numbers and where they had been seen.
Better not say anything, eh Gerrie!

After he reached the waders, the warblers, the island's own sub species of wren, and the final XYZs of the bird kingdom, he started on other animals.

'A porpoise seen from the Good Shepherd three miles north of Fair Isle,' said Neil, who was sitting at the front facing the audience.

'Don't tell me Neil, you're part of the entertainment too,' I joked, when he came over to see how our stomachs were doing.

'No, that's tomorrow night,' he replied smiling. 'I think David is tonight.'

David Wheeler was Fair Isle's weatherman. He had been sending regular meteorological reports down to the Met Office and the Shetland mainland for over twenty five years. I imagined it would have been on the basis of his reports that Radio 4 broadcast the Fair Isle bit of the Shipping Forecast. That evening he was there not as a meteorologist but as a photographer. He gave a great slide show of wonderful Fair Isle landscapes as an introduction to the island for the visitors. I was keen to

tell him what an influence he'd been, but as soon as the black bearded Dave finished his lecture he was off.
Probably fed up with nostalgic soothmoothers talking about the Shipping Forecast.

Before bed Gerrie and I studied the notice board and agreed what we'd like to do in the couple of days ahead of us.

'Neil's invited us all over for a drink to meet Pat before we leave,' she said.

'Fantastic. There's a guided walk tomorrow afternoon and I'd love to go and have a look at the knitting,'

'Don't get me started on the knitting,' Gerrie cooed.

The technique of using many bright colours so different from the naturally muted colours of the rest of Shetland became known as Fair Isle knitting because that is where it seemed to have developed. It has been suggested that there was a connection between the Fair Isle patterns and the historical event of the wrecking of Gran Griffon, a flagship of the Spanish Armada off Fair Isle. Another view was that the distinct style of the Fair Isle knitting has evolved over the centuries and took its patterns from many sources. The Armada cross was one variety as well as Norwegian stars like ice crystals and designs inspired by crofting life. Another influence was said to have been a kaleidoscope given as a gift to an islander at the turn of the twentieth century. For some years there had been a huge boom, with orders coming in for thousands of garments, and most knitters elsewhere in Shetland had to adopt the Fair Isle style of knitting.

'I see knitting as a symbol of oppression,' Gerrie said to Carla, the Italian textile tourist and myself at lunch on the second day of our stay.

'Please?' said Carla, who had been keen to be instructed in spinning and dying by one of the few remaining active members of the Fair Isle Knitters Cooperative.

'I remember as a wee child, maybe eighteen months old going to my mother for attention,' Gerrie said. 'It was always, 'not now.' The knitting always took priority over a cuddle. My mother was a single parent and was poorly paid on a piece by piece basis despite the skilled hours she would put in to producing complex garments. In earlier times, women knitted when they weren't doing other crofting work. The women's fingers were never allowed to be idle. Even as they walked to Church, they'd be knitting'

Carla and I nodded with interest.

'Yes, I can see what you mean. I had a Yell client, who was bullied at school so she avoided going. Nobody seemed to notice that most of her adolescence was spent in a corner of the croft house, knitting gloves. She missed out on her education and that affected her sense of self today,' I said.

What do you make of all that Carla? Perhaps it was one of those pair of her gloves that had kept my tiny hands warm in the big smogs of London in the early 1950s?

I kept all this in mind when Rhys and I went to have a look at the knitting but it didn't stop me souvenir hunting. It was a sparkling sunny day, perfect for strolling the couple of miles down towards the southern end of the island.

The bedroom of the Good Shepherd IV's Skipper was the showcase for the knitters' co-op. His wife had a few knitted garments displayed on the marital bed.

How game. I can't imagine inviting the whole world into our boudoir. I couldn't keep up with being tidy and clean all the time.

'A few days ago we had a cruise ship in so there's not much here,' the Skipper's wife proclaimed. 'We have orders for the next year or so,' she added, as she saw the disappointment in a tourist's face, who tried to squeeze into a smaller size sweater than she would have bought at M&S.

'I've been here for the past few days and before the cruise ship came in there was also very little,' said a passing tourist, as we stopped and chatted about our unsuccessful attempt to support one of the local economies.

'It's lack of Fair Isle knitters,' Pat, Neil's wife told us when we visited for a drink. 'The 'Fair Isle' brand is a registered trademark. That means that garments have to be knitted here. Although garments are machine knitted, they are hand finished and the hourly rate is still low for the complexity of the garments. Knitters on the island are diminishing. Young people aren't interested or don't have the time. Older knitters want to retire. It's a real dilemma.'

I had heard that there were under-employed knitters on the mainland.

Why don't they use their labour if they want to keep the industry alive? It sounds a bit like cutting off your nose to spite your face but perhaps it's more complicated.

Pat, an English woman had fallen with love with Neil when they had both worked for the Meteorological Office near Heathrow, over thirty years ago. Fair Isle was a National Trust territory, which meant that croft houses were all owned by the Trust and rented out on long-term lease to local people. Their croft had recently been given a makeover and we admired the NT's good taste of real wooden floors rather than the laminates that were tackily fashionable back home and which covered our own living room floor in Taffs Well. The Thompsons had decorated their croft with beautiful fabrics and tasteful furniture. As we sat sipping wine and chatting in the sophisticated ambiance, without looking out of the window at the ocean, you might have thought you were in the English Home Counties.

It was clear that Pat had thrown herself into Shetland life and was much loved by Neil's large extended family and the community. She had taken on a number of roles during her thirty years, from entrepreneur, marketer, knitter, teaching assistant to cleaner. Like Neil, the Second in command of the Good Shepherd IV and everyone else on Fair Isle, doing whatever job was required at the time. Pat showed us a wonderful photo of their 30th wedding anniversary. The whole island of 60 souls were in the photo. I even recognized one of the residents. David Wheeler's black beard stood out. Before I lost the chance I asked her the question that as an intoxicated ex-family mediator I'd been longing to ask.

'How do you settle disputes in a small community?'
What's that look Gerrie? Have I overstepped the mark?

It was after midnight when Neil offered to drive us back to the Observatory, which we gladly accepted. On the way out I noticed a range of outside coats. One donkey jacket with a bright orange shoulder piece read, 'Fireman,' another role to add to the list of his roles and talents, but that wasn't the last one I learnt about.

The following night Neil and his whole extended family assembled in the Observatory. They formed a band called 'Frideray' and entertained us with haunting tunes of emigration, loss, nostalgia and other bright sparky tunes, which got us all foot tapping. Neil's father played the fiddle, Neil played the guitar and his daughter sang solos. Other family members sang and played guitar, accordion and fiddle. Paulo, the Italian got down on the floor in contorted positions

to take close up shots of Neil's father; his crofting fingers fiddling.
It's been done Paulo. The 1970s are full of such photos.

That night I couldn't sleep. I lay in bed for hours, thinking about the people we had met, the mournful tunes wandering around my head. I got up and pulled the curtain back and gasped. A full moon shone on giant Sheep Rock painted black and rising majestically out of an illuminated sea of ink. I thought about crofters past who hauled their sheep up the sheer cliff face with ropes and pulleys to the small grassy slope which did for summer grazing.
Community is everything here. People are so resourceful and they only let new people in who have the skills they need. What a sense of identity and purpose. You have to sublimate your own ego to the common good. I'd be useless at it.
'Wake up Rhys, you can't miss this.'

The following morning we rose early and made our way down to North Haven to take the ferry back to Grutness. While the crew was loading I looked up the hill to see a young woman running down towards us.
'It's the warden's wife. Don't say we've left something behind. We did pay the bill, didn't we?" I said, already blaming Rhys for some unknown misdemeanour.

'I like to see guests off. I thought I'd overslept,' the tussled haired young woman said, as she approached panting.

'Do you see every ferry off?' I asked.

'I try to.'

As the Good Shepherd IV slipped out of the haven the Warden's wife waved us farewell from the quayside. Sheep Rock faded in a light mist.

As she got smaller, Frideray's tune, 'Faraway,' echoed in my head and I felt quite emotional.

'I feel like an émigré saying goodbye to my homeland and going off for a new life in Newfoundland,' I said turning to Rhys. I could see by his glazed look that he felt exactly the same.

'Sit down in the Skipper's chair if you like,' said Neil as we squeezed into the control cabin on board. The Skipper's gone down for a nap.'

I sat in the large black chair smiling like I'd just won the jackpot on Chris Tarrant's TV show, 'Who wants to be a millionaire?' I looked out at the fullness of the ocean. My year's ambition fulfilled.

'Well, didn't you say the sea was in your blood?' teased Neil. 'But don't worry, just to be on the safe side, I've put her on autopilot.'

'Oh No! It's the wedding photos,' said Rhys to the young woman in the newsagent come photo shop in Lerwick.

'I'm very sorry. You can have a full refund,' she said, after conferring with the boss.

'Something happened to the family's video camera at the wedding and ours were the only photos taken of the couple from the balcony,' I muttered.

'It's never happened before. I've brought lots of films in here for developing. Why does the machine have to mangle this film now? It's irreplaceable.'

'I am really sorry. Look, you can have the next film you have developed here free of charge.'
He thinks we're coming back?

The previous Friday Calum Andrews's son had married his sweetheart at Scalloway Methodist Church. When I came up for the interview the year before, Calum had taken me on a spin to see a bit of Shetland before making my mind up about the job. Chatting in the car we exchanged information about our children. His son was only seventeen then but he and his girl were very keen to get hitched, but had agreed to wait until they were both eighteen, when they hoped to go to university together as a married couple. In his wise way Calum played it cool offering support and advice as and when it was asked for. The couple it seemed never faltered in their intentions and on that Friday in August Rhys and I were fortunate to be invited to their wedding.

It was a blustery day. The airy restored church, stood on the sea front, the spot from where the Shetland Bus had left on its dangerous missions to and from Norway in World War 2. We went upstairs for a good view and were ideally placed to take some birds' eye snaps of the couple including some of the bride's beautifully appliquéd dress splayed out around her. Calum's clan were from Fife and all the men sported their tartan with pride. He confessed that it had taken his wife a couple of trips down south to find the right outfit. She looked wonderful and with the other women in the groom's family blended harmoniously in a range of pink, violet and lavender like a Munro in autumn. It is not a Shetland tradition to wear the kilt but the bride's family, long established Shetlanders, were suited and booted in their best. The church was packed with their friends and family and it was a very happy event.

'Don't take any photos of me greetin',' said Calum, who unexpectedly didn't blubber his way through the whole service as we all predicted. Although, I have to admit that the whole congregation had a bit of a greet when the psalm about love was recited and Calum's sister sang to the couple.

Even more people attended the evening do. The community hall in Scalloway was heaving. On the way in we queued with other guests for a dram of whisky and a piece of wedding cake and then looked around for somewhere out of the spotlight to sit and enjoy the evening. It was hard to find anywhere so we slid in by the stage, where a fiddle band was in full swing. The dancing was started by the bride and groom, who were competitive and accomplished folk dancers. They did a kind of Gay Gordon around the hall. Every time they circled the hall, another couple joined and followed the dance, starting with their families, then close friends, then everyone else, until almost everyone who had been seated was up on their feet and following in line. That was everyone except the disabled, the hard of hearing, and us of course.

Music is so intrinsic to the lives of Shetlanders and music was on offer everywhere. Pubs in Lerwick such as 'The Lounge' and 'Da Noost' had regular live artists and encouraged audience participation. People got together to jam together on a weekly basis such as the jam we had attended at Tingwall Golf Club, when Rachel came up in February. There was a Blues festival in July and an annual folk festival in September, which we had missed last year, arriving too late and would miss that year, leaving beforehand. 'Fiddle Frenzy' had recently become an annual event in August, where local and international fiddlers come for a week, doing workshops and concerts. The fiddle was the most popular instrument in Shetland, being taught at schools to a high level. Also popular was the guitar and the accordion.

Pity that neither Rhys nor I played an instrument. It would have offered a lot of fun and chance to become more part of that community.

Lerwick's Leisure Centre was packed when we took our seats for the 'Fiddle Frenzy' final concert, the culmination of the week's events. 'Fiddlers Bid' a band of six or more young men, some from Shetland themselves, got their audience into a pitch of unbridled excitement. It was the best live folk concert I had ever attended and we were up on our feet with the rest of the audience stamping and braying for more.

September was calling, ever closer. Endings were starting to appear like cracks in a newly plastered wall. The worse summer since 1942 and autumn already in the air. We wanted to go home but weren't quite ready to leave. There were still places we wanted to visit, events we wanted to attend.

Wednesday the 18th of August was my last day at Whalsay Health centre. Whalsay had remained my favourite place of work. Whalsay was also known as the 'The Bonny Isle,' and I had found the Whalsay folk very bonny. Freya, of course was also originally from Whalsay. Although I only saw clients there every fortnight I felt more part of the team than I did at Lerwick. Dr Suzanne Ward had taken over from the previous GP, who had recently retired after thirty years work. The appreciative community had showered him with presents including a gold watch and a foreign holiday. Suzanne had been a locum on Unst for several years and I had got to know her there. She was supportive of the counselling service and gave me good feedback on my work.

Chrissie, the practice manager and Janet her assistant gave me gifts and a thank you card. I guess they must have appreciated my efforts to counsel in the kitchenette.

'I'll miss your accent,' I said hugging them both.

'What do you mean?' said Janet. 'All year I've been speaking to you in my best English!

Over the year we had taken the ferry together, Rhys taking advantage of his pensioner's transport concession, and as I went off to the Health Centre he went off sightseeing, sketching and taking photos. On the last day I finished early and he showed me some of the places I'd missed.

On that last occasion we stopped to take a look at the Pier House, a Hansa German merchant house and store from the seventeenth century. Trading between Shetland and Germany has taken place for over 300 years. Its inhabitants had always depended on the sea for a living. Whalsay men had taken part in the Haaf fishing in large rowing boats and in the herring boom, but it was only after World War 2 that development really started and since then a large fleet of modern vessels, all owned by their crews formed a large part of Shetland's fishing industry. As we stood on the deck of the ferry taking us back to the mainland I savoured every moment that I could keep Whalsay in view.

At the end of August the counselling team and their partners took Rhys and I out for a farewell meal at Raba. After the meal they presented us with a photo by Coutts, a local photographer, of two courting puffins and gave me an unusual amethyst coloured necklace to match the earrings they had given me for my birthday.

Other presents included engraved glasses from Unst, chocolates, and a Shetland silver brooch of three swans.

My clients gave me cards and presents. One ex-client even took me out for lunch at a restaurant that I had been wanting to eat at all year. Freya invited me to her house for lunch. Maggie and Bob, Gerrie and Joe had us over for farewell meals. We were treated with great affection and generosity but at the time it was hard to believe that we were really leaving.

Fence Post Warning

September 2005

September 2nd was my last day in work for the Shetland Health Board. I went around the Lerwick Health Centre and Montfield saying goodbyes to staff. I felt like I'd just arrived. They probably felt the same. Calum had once said to me that when he wanted to run away from somewhere that it was often from an inner place of hurt. I didn't feel I was running away from a place of hurt any longer. I had faced that place of hurt eye ball to eye ball. It was still there but it was smaller and more manageable. I had much to thank Freya for the work she had done with me in this respect. I hadn't yet cracked the issue of belonging and it would still take me some time to make sense of this whole Shetland experience.

I couldn't ascertain how common it was for incomers like me to leave after such a short time working in Shetland. Nobody in the Shetland Health Board (SHB) was that forthcoming with information. The relocation package was generous and if you stayed for two years you didn't have to pay anything back, but if less than two years there was a sliding scale of repayment. We hadn't used much of the allocation as we hadn't bought a property so we didn't have much to pay back.

As long as there is a shortage of skills and experience in an area I guess there will always be a need to import labour. At the time that I was recruited there were few equally qualified and experienced indigenous counsellors. That was changing. As I was leaving a new cohort of graduates from the College diploma course in counselling and psychotherapy was emerging. Calum decided to advertise locally for a replacement and two people, one a Shetlander and the other a soothmoother, who had worked in Shetland for several years, were appointed as part-timers, rather than full time. This gave the service more flexibility.

A number of Shetlanders had said to us that they felt that the SHB advertisement offering a paradise life style was misleading. Yes, Shetland could offer everything it described, 'the pollution free environment, the fresh fish, good education and leisure facilities' and a great place to bring up a young family. There were other things that needed to be mentioned somewhere, colleagues said, like the remoteness, the gales in winter, possible loneliness, and the journey time back home. In fact, Calum brought up all those things when after the interview we spent a diamond bright day together driving around the mainland. It made no difference. I fell in love with Shetland the moment I landed and I was set on coming.

The Human Resources department of SHB gave me an exit interview and I told them all this. I did suggest what might help new soothmoothers was a 'buddy scheme,' where an incomer could be paired up with a local family, who could be a source of support, introduction and local information in the first few months. We were very lucky. The counselling team had been fantastic and the introduction we had to Maggie and Bob gave us an excellent social outlet outside of work. But without Rhys to support me and share the experience I wonder if I would have even made half a year? I think that I may have been just too lonely. Perhaps it is easier when you're younger, like it had been for me when I did VSO all those years ago. Or, maybe it just takes time and you have to give it more time than we were prepared to. The pull of our family and home was just too great.

In the next week Rhys attempted to visit Foula by 'The Islander,' but the weather was always poor at the times of scheduled flights. Instead, in a short break in the weather he managed to see Papa Stour from the air, which he relished taking lots of photos to show me. We revisited the places we loved, walked in places we hadn't been to before, said our goodbyes again to our friends and neighbours and then before we knew it we were packing our old Peugeot Estate to its gills with the contents of our wardrobes and the garden shed.

'I'll be greetin' down at the promontory near the Amenities Trust. Make sure you look out for me,' said Calum, as I popped in one last time to say goodbye. Emily texted me from Brae saying that although she couldn't be there physically she'd be there in spirit with Calum. Tracy had already left the isles for a holiday down south.

It was a greyish afternoon on September the 9th, as we drove onto the Hrossey, the sky Turner-esque with a watery pomegranate glow. The days were shortening, it was getting colder and the sun timed its setting appropriately as the ferry pulled out of Lerwick taking us on our final journey down south and home. We huddled together on the top deck breathing in the salty remains of the Lerwick day. As the ferry mooched alongside the town we suddenly saw Calum.

'There he is,' blurted Rhys, his eyes glistening.

A solitary figure stood against a small red car waving a blue shirt-sleeved arm.

'Can he see us?' I choked, as I waved furiously. 'Keep waving, Rhys! Keep waving!'

***

Only time in the sea!

Post Script, July 2015

I finished *Shetland Saga* with the assistance of Susan Richardson in early 2008. My apologies to friends who visited us in Shetland and didn't get a mention, particularly, Elizabeth and Colin, Elin, and Janice. We really did appreciate your visits. We did also make a visit to Orkney during our stay but have not included that trip in this book. Apologies to Orcadians!

I submitted my draft to the script reading service of the then Academi (now Literature Wales) for feedback and comment. They made various suggestions as to how it could be made more exciting including re-shaping it into a series of incidents/happenings rather than a chronological diary. I decided not to do that as I wrote the book primarily for myself, family and friends. I hope that the chronological diary shows how I struggled with certain issues over the year and how I worked through them with Rhys and the help of Calum, Freya, my colleagues and friends. I left my draft on the shelf and only recently, seven years later, have been persuaded by friends to return to it and consider self-publishing. This I am doing with the aid of Dave Lewis, a writer, poet and photographer who also helps other writers self-publish.

After returning to Taffs Well in 2005 Calum Andrews agreed to become my clinical supervisor and has done so for nearly ten years. Managers cannot be their employee's clinical supervisors while in employment but once the relationship changes it becomes possible. Thus I have been able to draw on the expertise and friendship of this highly accomplished professional for the past decade. We recently agreed it was time for a change.

Since 2006 I have had a small but successful private practice, counselling from home and working with a range of issues. I particularly enjoy working with couples experiencing difficulties in their relationship. This has brought together my counselling and mediation skills. I have developed professional and personal interest in early attachment theory and how it plays out in adult relationships and its links to neurological research.

Rhys and I are still together. I continue to be amazed at what he puts up with and am very grateful for his continuing support. Since then we've done lots of trips together, including our first cruise - a Saga cruise, that I've also written about. As you can imagine the experience was not straightforward! We have both had hip replacements, he has had other health issues but presently we are very fortunate to be well and mobile.

We have grown closer creatively as artist and writer. Our friend Frida's prophesy has come about as my passion for writing has developed. I have attended numerous creative writing classes, written poetry, plays, short stories, started a novel, chaired a script writing group, kept a blog and recently set up a local creative writing group. But I have had very little work published. Over the last ten years that has become increasingly less important than the pleasure, challenge, stimulation and therapeutic benefits I have had from the process of writing. I now even offer writing as part of my therapeutic range with clients.

In addition Rhys and I have embarked on three creative projects resulting in joint exhibitions of his art work and my writing. They have been on the theme of our dreams and nightmares, celebrations of nature and the impact of climate change, and a celebration of the Pembrokeshire landscape. We've focused on our own creativity, sparked off by one another's ideas, beliefs and imagery. In doing this we've raised some funds through the sale of Rhys' paintings for the homeless, miners' families, local environmental projects and Friends of the Earth.

We haven't forgotten our Shetland Friends and they have been wonderful at not forgetting us. Since ending therapy Freya, the art therapist, has become a close friend and we are in fairly regular email contact. Gerrie I hear from less often but every Christmas for the past ten years she has sent us a whole Shetland smoked salmon. Maggie and Bob we hear from less often too but they also don't forget us at Christmas time. Sadly, Donald died tragically a few years ago.

What of our children? Our daughter Rachel has a successful career teaching. She's worked in some tough schools in Wales and London, and in a top notch college in Singapore. She is currently deputy in a large English department in a comprehensive school. She is married and expecting her first child. Liam, our son, finished university, later went on to do a masters, and has just graduated with a doctorate. He is working as a senior design engineer with an international company in Switzerland, and still a keen mountain biker and snowboarder.

As Maggie warned they've gone off and done their own thing. So do I have any regrets about leaving Shetland so soon? No. It was the right decision. Although Rachel lives in London we can offer her some support as a young Mum that we would not have been able to do from the Northern Isles, and Switzerland is only an hour or so away from Heathrow. Becoming grandparents is the start of a whole new adventure!

We now look back on that year in Shetland as a watershed. It enabled us to grow and develop as individuals, as a couple and a family. I often thank Calum Andrews for making it possible. It was a remarkable experience and even more appreciated in retrospect.

Wales is a wonderful country to live and work in and I now appreciate what we have here more than I ever thought possible before Shetland.

JTD, July 2015.

Looking West

Bibliography

Graham, John J The Shetland Dictionary, Shetland Times, 2004.

Harrap, Hugh Where to watch birds in Shetland, Harrap, 2000.

Raban, Jonathan The Oxford Book of the sea. OUP, 1993.

Reader's Digest. Book of British Birds

Rough Guides Scotland, 1988.

Rough Guides Scottish Highlands and Islands, 2002.
Schei, Livkjorsvik & Moberg. The Shetland Story, Batsford, 1988.

Shetland Times Weekly Newspaper

Shetland Times Shetland Visitor, 2005.

Tait, Charles The Shetland Guide. Charles Tait Photographic, 2003.

Tait, Charles The Souvenir Guide to Orkney. 2nd ed. Charles Tait, 200?

Telford, Susan In a world a wirane: a Shetland Herring Girl's story. S.T, 1988.

Welsh, Mary Walking Shetland. Clan Books, 2004.

To read more about our comings and goings see my blog - http://janetdaniel-writer.blogspot.com

See also Rhys' website –
http://ieuanrhysdaniel.tumblr.com

Also available as an e-book from Amazon.

For more information on self-publishing visit –
www.publishandprint.co.uk

Printed in Great Britain
by Amazon.co.uk, Ltd.,
Marston Gate.